PUERILITIES

THE LOCKERT LIBRARY OF POETRY IN TRANSLATION
EDITORIAL ADVISOR: RICHARD HOWARD

For other titles in the Lockert Library, see p. 125

PUERILITIES

Erotic Epigrams of
The Greek Anthology

TRANSLATED BY
DARYL HINE

PRINCETON UNIVERSITY PRESS
PRINCETON AND OXFORD

Published by Princeton University Press, 41 William Street, Princeton,
New Jersey 08540
In the United Kingdom: Princeton University Press, 3 Market Place,
Woodstock, Oxfordshire OX20 1SY

Translations of *Strato,* I, CC, CCVI, CCVII, and CCXLII; *Meleager,* XCV
and CXXII; *Rhianos,* XCIII; *Diodes,* IV; *Anonymous,* XVII and CXLV;
Scythinus, XXII; and *Glaucus,* XLIV, originally appeared in the *Columbia
Anthology of Gay Literature* and are used here by kind permission of the
editor, Byrne R. S. Fone.

Library of Congress Cataloging-in-Publication Data
Greek anthology. Book 12. English
Puerilities : erotic epigrams of The Greek anthology / translated by
Daryl Hine.
p. cm. — (Lockert library of poetry in translation)
Includes bibliographical references and index.
ISBN 0-691-08819-5 (alk. paper) — ISBN 0-691-08820-9 (pbk. : alk paper)
1. Erotic poetry, Greek—Translations into English.   2. Epigrams, Greek—
Translations into English.   I. Hine, Daryl.   II. Title.   III. Series.
PA3624.E75 P84 2001
881′.010803538—dc21   00-066885

This book has been composed in Adobe Garamond

The paper used in this publication meets the minimum requirements of
ANSI/NISO Z39.48-1992 (R 1997) (*Permanence of Paper*)

www.pup.princeton.edu

Printed in the United States of America
10 9 8 7 6 5 4 3 2 1

The Lockert Library of Poetry in Translation is supported by
a bequest from Charles Lacy Lockert (1888–1974)

For Jerry

You mavericks, what language should explain
The derivation of the word makes plain:
Boy-lovers, Dionysius, love boys—
You can't deny it—not great hobblehoys.
After I referee the Pythian
Games, you umpire the Olympian:
The failed contestants I once sent away
You welcome as competitors today.

CONTENTS

INTRODUCTION

THE TWELFTH book of *The Greek Anthology* compiled at the court of Hadrian in the second century A.D. by a poetaster Straton, who like most anthologists included an immodest number of his own poems, is itself a part of a larger collection of short poems dating from the dawn of Greek lyric poetry (Alcaeus) down to its last florescence, which survived two Byzantine recensions to end up in a single manuscript in the library of the Count Palatine in Heidelberg—hence its alternative title, *The Palatine Anthology,* usually abbreviated to *Anth. Pal.* This particular, indeed special, collection contained in Book XII subtitled *The Musa Paedika* or *Musa Puerilis,* alternately from the Greek word for a child of either sex— and girls are not wholly absent from these pages—or the Latin for "boy," consists of 258 epigrams on various aspects of Boy Love or, to recur to the Greek root, paederasty. Some of these poems are by the greatest poets of the Greek language, such as Alcaeus and Callimachus; many are by less well known but nonetheless polished writers, such as Meleager, Asclepiades, Rhianus, and Strato himself; many, these not the least worthy, are anonymous. Their tone varies from the lighthearted and bawdy to the grave and resigned. The overall effect is one of witty wistfulness rather than rampant, reciprocated lust, of longing—what the Greeks called *pothos*— rather than satisfaction, and also of regret. As happy, let alone domestic, love has occasioned very little poetry at any time, as passion almost always sounds a plaintive note—here at least seldom rising into the desperate wail we hear, for example in Catullus— we might well seek an explanation in the nature of desire itself, on the Platonic model envisaging a forever unattainable, divine object, of which all earthly affection is merely a mirror, however delightful and sometimes delusive. That this undercurrent of spiritual *pothos* is far from conscious in these poems needs no comment; but it is implicit in the very nature of Love or Eros itself—or, as so often familiarly personified, Himself.

That the objects of such passion were masculine and for the most part at least comparatively juvenile is an historical fact and, like all facts, an accident. The fact that other later poets in another though not wholly dissimilar Christian, heterosexual tradition, such as notably Dante, Petrarch, Chrétien de Troyes, and Goethe, to mention only a few, found transcendence in the eternal feminine instead is also of but incidental interest. Fashions in passion change, like fads in anything else, and while we are given to thinking our own modes and norms of conduct both universal and solely acceptable, the merest glance at history, literature, and anthropology will show us otherwise, as will a peep behind the façade of respectable behavior. The family unit, however defined, is itself a comparatively recent invention or convention; for whereas the bond of mother and child remains for our kind as for each of us the earliest form of attachment, among adults—and we should never forget that adulthood began much earlier in earlier times—it was the group, the horde, or that most decried yet most prevalent group, the gang. Gangs, first I suppose for hunting game, are to be found not only on streetcorners but in board rooms, the most common and powerful type of the gang being the committee. The group for and within which these poems were composed and circulated was neither a gang nor a committee—itself a martial term originally—but a court, neither an academy nor yet an institute; these rather than those high-flown heterosexual fantasies of the twelfth century represented the first form quite literally of courtly love.

Love, surrounded by the simpering Graces,
And Bacchus are ill-suited to straight faces.

Love, love, love, Eros, personified and impersonal, bitter yet sweet, now an infant on his mother's lap, now an adolescent boy winged with fanciful desires and armed with the playthings of youth, his arrows less fatal than those of Apollo and Artemis but also less painless, inflicting an incurable festering wound, is the paramount deity and pervasive, prevalent spirit of these poems. Even almighty Zeus is seldom mentioned save as the grasping, aquiline lover of Ganymede, the paradigmatic catamite. Eros at this period, always, at least in his origins, physical, figured as Aphrodite's son, fatherless, older in some respects than She, urge or demiurge, impulse and illusion, never absent yet often unnamed in these lines, prevails: *Amor omnia vincit.* Yet love not only conquers; he, she, or it oppresses, teases, and torments. Unfavorably compared by some flattering suitors to certain of his lovelier mortal incarnations, Eros is sometimes also said to suffer from the passion he provokes. From time to time, if only hopefully, the tables may be turned on the mischievous little monster, in a role reversal with obvious implications:

> This is the boy to be enamored of,
> Young men, a new love superior to Love.
>
> LIX [Meleager]

> Thief of hearts, why jettison your cruel
> Arrows and bow and, weeping, fold your wings?
> Invincible Myiscus' looks must fuel
> Repentance for your previous philanderings.
>
> CXLIV [Meleager]

Our modern sense of such things is if anything more graphic, yet we will ask in vain what, exactly, these people did, sexwise. Ambiguous hints and metaphors are all we are given. The divine yet very real generative impulse—for the notion of an immaterial divinity, though hardly unknown, if as mathematically conceived by

Plato, seemed altogether strange to popular religion and our authors alike, at once down to earth and highfalutin—infallibly overwhelms both its object and its vessel, even as it informs its verbal medium. The sentiments of these juvenescent expressions are, within a persistent convention alien to us, as conventional as those on any Valentine card, though more ingeniously and frankly couched.

Besides Eros himself and his mother, the divinized entities most mentioned are Dionysus (Bacchus)—Drink—and the Graces, physical and social, surrounding and supporting Beauty.

Alcoholic beverages, best known in the form of wine to the peoples of ancient Greece (though some, like Callimachus as resident of Ptolemaic Egypt, might have been familiar with the ancient Egyptians' everyday liquid refreshment, beer), were, like everything else important to life, celebrated as the gifts of god and were themselves godly. The ancients had no specific designation, unless Eros himself, for life or the life force. On the other hand they did pay realistic if reluctant homage to the gods of the underworld, beginning with Zeus' brother Hades, once or twice mentioned here with other animistic deities of sea and land. Yet we would be wrong, I believe, in imagining such beings or concepts as wholly allegorical. They were very real, often attached to a real or imaginary place as Zeus was to Olympus or the sky; the Muses, themselves established on or near Olympus as well as on the mountains or hills they were thought to frequent, were, with the Graces and Hours, part of that wider, more ancient, and originally local class of beings, the nymphs who lived in trees and water, and all the other many divine beings of fresh water and salt, Poseidon, Thetis, Amphitrite, and the rest—not all feminine—so that the ancients inhabited a world itself divine where every act and substance had divine import, at a time when Christianity was a cheerless underground sect repudiating all these beings under their accepted names, while retaining in the Sacrament the transubstantial elements of Wine and Bread, Dionysus and Ceres.

Of course gods could be created as well as accepted; the most striking example at the period in question being, perhaps beside the divinized wonderworker from Palestine Himself, Antinous, the beloved of Hadrian, who stood in relation to him as Ganymede to Zeus or Hyacinth to Apollo. Posthumously decreed divine honors, like many of the Roman emperors, and worshipped by imperial decree throughout the empire, Antinous abides as the type of the *eromenos,* absent in name but present by association and implication throughout these pages.

A CONDITION also implicit here though unnamed, slavery, was as universal in the world in question as paederasty. Some but certainly not all of these desirable lads were slaves, as is clear in this verse by the anthologist himself, the least sentimental of boy-lovers:

> Were you a novice I'd tried to persuade
> To vice, you might be right to be afraid;
> But since your master's bed taught you a lot,
> Why not treat someone else to what you've got?
> Called to your post, your duty done, without
> A word, your sleepy master throws you out.
> But here are other pleasures, free speech and
> Fun by solicitation not command.
>
> CCXI [Strato]

But such are the rules, indeed the reality, of such attachments that it is the lover not the beloved who is enslaved, even when, as often seems to have been the case, the boy is a whore. Strato, again:

> What now, my pet, depressed, in tears again?
> What do you want? Don't torture me! Speak plain.
> You hold your palm out! I'm disgusted at
> Your asking payment. Where did you learn that?

Seed cakes and conkers will not make you merry
Now, that your mind has grown so mercenary.
I curse the customer with his perverse
Lessons who made my little rascal worse!

The object of such love is always, his civil state notwithstanding, free and generally elusive. Therefore the character of his actual condition, whether slave or not, is never mentioned, as it is in fact irrelevant. A very great man once said, when asked what he thought of Free Love, that if it wasn't free it wasn't love. And so we find it here; any enslavement is that of the lover and like so much in these poems, half imaginary, even voluntary, willful. A convention as much as a predicament, playful even when despondent, the affection and desire of an older man for a younger though frequently far from hopeless, must be tinged as so many of these poems are with a resigned sadness, sometimes amounting to bitter consciousness of evanescence. As youth is the indispensable desideratum of paederasty—although in several verses the loves of young boys for each other are mentioned—it is naturally fleeting, almost immaterial, while of course evinced by specified physical traits. "Just wait," the poet-lover seems to say, "soon you will be as old and unattractive as I, but never so clever." The generation gap will be closed when it is too late. If, as more than one unsympathetic critic has complained, all this is mere "high-school stuff"—surely more current in private than public schools? (though even there such arrangements and derangements are not unknown) and doubtless in other all male institutions—we may be sure that the epigrams, written for boys of school age, were composed rather by their elders, masters, or teachers. Moreover it is also likely that, no matter whom they were ostensibly addressed to, their actual audience would have been the authors' coevals and/or colleagues, other older poets and lovers. The lads here named, many of them not altogether illiterate (cf. CLXXXVII), may never have read or even heard their praise, dispraise, and gratuitous, unwanted, and probably unacceptable advice.

As TO the diction, benedictions, or maledictions of the epigrams, which I have tried to carry over into English, let me make a few preliminary perhaps premonitory remarks. The Greeks, like us, spoke not just one language but several, often without knowing so. Poets in particular, wishing to exploit all the possibilities of their language—and a poet can only convincingly write in his native tongue, however elaborated or diluted by education—can either stick to what they suppose is standard speech, or, like Shakespeare, vary their discourse for surprising but appropriate effect. Goethe said that anachronism was the essence of poetry, and it plays a great part in the different kinds of diction that meld, both in everyday usage and in poetic contrivance, into what we perceive as comprehensible if sometimes odd if not inappropriate language. Anachronism, by the way, is merely a form of paradox, truly a basic poetical resource as well as a logical one, and much in play here— as, for instance, in the conception of the sweet bitterness or the bitter sweetness of love.

Without embarking on the complexities of Greek dialects, from the earliest times in which every city, then every area, spoke its own peculiar form of what was still recognizably the same language, to the latest period when on one level the vulgar spoke what is called *koiné* ("common"), the language of the New Testament, whereas the better educated had also their own less common and reductionist but even more ostentatiously mixed lingo or "linqua franca et jocundissima," one might simply observe that the main language groups were all employed in poetry, each according to an of course unwritten convention by which, for instance, Ionic, the language of Homer and Hesiod (with even at that early date some admixtures), was reserved for epic, Aeolic for melic or lyric verse (after Sappho and Alcaeus), and Doric or Boeotion for bucolics, like those of Theocritus, Moschus, and Bion. Attic was used primarily for prose and the stichomythic dialogues of tragedy: but while there was a Muse of tragedy—Calliope—there could not be one for prose, as that highly evolved and artificial literary form so long antedated the conception of the Muses, daughters of Mnemosyne or memory; it seems no accident that while the fundamental excuse for verse is its memorability, prose is scarcely memorable at all—as any schoolchild forced to memorize the Gettysburg Address or the speeches of Tacitus or Cicero will attest. Let us just agree that the language of the poems in the *Anthology* is more or less a mish-mash, like that of this paragraph.

One peculiar dictionary challenge in some of these poems is their use of words that, while we might regard them as obscene, or at best impolite, the Greeks may well not have. Obscenity is a result of repression, and it is difficult to see signs of repression anywhere in Greek life or art. The terms in question, some unique—*hapax legomena*—particularly in the many poems (too many, really) by Strato, the perhaps self-appointed court poet of Hadrian, are simple, crude, incomprehensible except in context, and like all such language, in essence childish. For what we repress, while hardy forgetting it, is much of our childhood along with its vocabulary of *pee-pee* and *kaka*. In the case of one poem (III) in which these terms are exploited for comic effect, I have used the commonest counterparts in English—fortunately at last printable. For further elucidation the reader may consult lexica in vain, but for the many mythological references should have recourse to Bullfinch's (or as I like to call it, Bullfeather's) *Mythology*.

Oral poetry was the primary means of communication in this old world, besides conversation, but written prose was a late invention brought to its highest perfection by Plato. Prose must by definition be written down, whereas poetry was for ages meant to be memorized or extemporized and recited: one may easily imagine these epigrams being bandied about at symposia, dinners, and drinking parties, again, for men only. Few people could write, and some of those, like Vergil, did not care to, and would dictate their verses, as blind Milton and in our day Jorge Luis Borges did out of necessity. The dissemination and dilution of literacy in our time has led not to a wider let alone a deeper appreciation of the best efforts of the past and present, but to a widespread appetite for and consumption of tripe. The poems in *The Greek Anthology,* admittedly trivial, are not tripe. Literature owes as much to illiteracy as it does to blindness; Homer (probably a misnomer) was reputed both blind and preliterate. We are fortunate, since as it is said, *littera scripta manet,* "the written letter remains so," that The *Odyssey* as well as these fugitive, occasional pieces were written and copied and edited. Aratus, one of the light-versifiers here included, also edited Homer, as did Callimachus and Apologies Rhodes, and wrote, besides other, lost works, a poem on astronomy, *Phaenomena.* The pre-Socratic were not the only serious and speculative persons to commit their lucubrations to verse: Lucretius' *De Rerum Natura* may be mentioned, derived largely from the prose writings of the earlier post-Socratic, prose philosopher Epicurus. Epicureanism in its more popular sense, rather than Stoicism pervades the poems of the *Musa Paedika.* Though it is tempting to think of prose as Stoic and poetry as Epicurean, this is not in fact always so.

Oral—and aural—verse, which is to say virtually all poetry written before the last and, as far as literature is concerned, rather lamentable century, just what is still generally regarded as poetry, and which still manifests itself in popular music, for instance "rap," at once rhymed, rhythmical, and as extemporaneous as jazz, has its own unspoken rules and rights-of-way.

The metrical form of the originals I have rather represented than slavishly imitated, as I tried to in my purely accentual dactylic versions of the *Idylls* of Theocritus (Atheneum, 1982), *The Homeric Hymns* (Atheneum, 1972), and Hesiod's *Works and Days* and *Theogony* (University of Chicago Press, 2000). There the form was stichic, and as seemed to befit unrhymed single lines following each other in ever varied succession, I have used not the commonest, indeed only ordinary such stichic English meter, blank verse, but chose to echo the sound of the Greek more directly, allowing for the differences beween quantitative and stressed verse (the ambiguities and subtleties of which would require a larger and longer digression than this short preface would allow) in six stressed lines, basically dactylic but permitting as much spondaic pseudo-resolution as the matter suggested and our language permits. The predominant, almost the only, form here is not stichic but strophic: an unrhymed couplet repeated ad libitum, consisting of the commonest meter in Greek and Latin, the dactylic hexameter, followed by a line composed of its first two feet, plus one syllable, of that metrical unit the so-called hemieps, repeated, thus forming the second most popular classical unit, the elegiac couplet, which may be roughly thumped out thus:

> tumpidy tumpidy tumpidy tumpidy tumpidy tumtum
> tumpidy tumpidy tum tumpidy tumpidy tum

Replacing the longum with an ictus—the long syllable with a stressed one—we would get something like the following English elegiac couplet:

> Nor are some authors the only anonymous blooms in this
>   garland:
> Most of the boys might as well be heteronymous too.

While this seems not only fairly accurate as representation, but not unpleasing, the effect, much-repeated, is rather sedative than, as an epigram should be, piquant, surprising and evocative, in its basic sense of a wake-up call. Therefore the reader should do as I did after much experimentation with the above model: more or less abandon it altogether in favor of a more familiar native meter, the rhymed couplet or quatrain, such as I used to represent the elegiac couplets in Ovid's *Heroines* (Yale, 1991). Rhyme, though it certainly does exist in Greek as in all languages in the crudest manifestation as assonance and consonance, was not deployed unless for special, subliminal effect (see the rhyming pun in Callimachus: XLIII); the morphology of the language made terminal rhyme, which is all most of us hear as rhyme at all, undesirable as too easy: hence all these quantitative evasions thereof.

The language into which a poem is translated must be of more interest and importance to the reader of that language than the original tongue, and certainly should be so to the translator. A verse translation is not merely a trot or paraphrase of the original; to succeed it should, and must, be a wholly convincing and pleasurable poetic experience in its own right. Therefore guided by Aristotle's criterion of effect above all, I have plumped for what I deem the most effective means of simulacry, as shown in my versions. In a few cases I thought the tone and subject matter more suited to a limerick form than the staider couplet: as the limerick is the most popular indeed vulgar verse form in contemporary usage, it seemed to fit some of this badinage better. Here I might offer the reader two versions of the same elegiac couplet and ask him or her to chose a preference, if he or she can:

    V   STRATO

Pale skins I like, but honey-colored more,
And blond and brunette boys I both adore.
I never blackball brown eyes, but above
All, eyes of scintillating black I love.

[Limerick]
Are pale skins my favorite, or
Honey-hued adolescents? What is more,
    Liking blond and brunette,
    I love brown eyes—and yet
Scintillating black eyes I adore.

As I am no textual scholar but a poet who knows which texts make sense and are aesthetically preferable I shall abbreviate a long excursion into the wilderness of textualism by thanking the Muse—here Erato, for the ancients had muses for everything, even for smut—for preserving this bouquet of real and artificial flowers in a comparatively unified and simplified form. In the case of rare lacunae and gaps in the text I have silently bridged the gap, remembering that asyndeton and non sequiturs are also rhetorical devices. Throughout, my aim has been not archaeological but almost authorial, to produce rather than reproduce with all the resources of our resourceful language, something that I hope will surpass a mere simulacrum. I trust that these epigrams, so often but pleasantries, will stand as valid poems in their own light: not symphonies like the Homeric poets and all their imitators, but bagatelles.

PUERILITIES

I ΣΤΡΑΤΩΝΟΣ

Ἐκ Διὸς ἀρχώμεσθα, καθὼς εἴρηκεν Ἄρατος·
ὑμῖν δ᾽, ὦ Μοῦσαι, σήμερον οὐκ ἐνοχλῶ.
εἰ γὰρ ἐγὼ παῖδάς τε φιλῶ καὶ παισὶν ὁμιλῶ,
τοῦτό τι πρὸς Μούσας τὰς Ἑλικωνιάδας;

II ΣΤΡΑΤΩΝΟΣ

Μὴ ζήτει δέλτοισιν ἐμαῖς Πρίαμον παρὰ βωμοῖς,
μηδὲ τὰ Μηδείης πένθεα καὶ Νιόβης,
μηδ᾽ Ἴτυν ἐν θαλάμοις, καὶ ἀηδόνας ἐν πετάλοισιν·
ταῦτα γὰρ οἱ πρότεροι πάντα χύδην ἔγραφον·
ἀλλ᾽ ἱλαραῖς Χαρίτεσσι μεμιγμένον ἡδὺν Ἔρωτα,
καὶ Βρόμιον· τούτοις δ᾽ ὀφρύες οὐκ ἔπρεπον.

III ΣΤΡΑΤΩΝΟΣ

Τῶν παίδων, Διόδωρε, τὰ προσθέματ᾽ εἰς τρία πίπτει
σχήματα, καὶ τούτων μάνθαν᾽ ἐπωνυμίας.
τὴν ἔτι μὲν γὰρ ἄθικτον ἀκμὴν λάλου ὀνόμαζε,
κωκὼ τὴν φυσᾶν ἄρτι καταρχομένην·
τὴν δ᾽ ἤδη πρὸς χεῖρα σαλευομένην, λέγε σαύραν·
τὴν δὲ τελειοτέρην, οἶδας ἃ χρή σε καλεῖν.

IV ΣΤΡΑΤΩΝΟΣ

Ἀκμῇ δωδεκέτους ἐπιτέρπομαι· ἔστι δὲ τούτου
χὠ τρισκαιδεκέτης πουλὺ ποθεινότερος·
χὠ τὰ δὶς ἑπτὰ νέμων, γλυκερώτερον ἄνθος Ἐρώτων·
τερπνότερος δ᾽ ὁ τρίτης πεντάδος ἀρχόμενος·
ἐξεπικαιδέκατον δὲ θεῶν ἔτος· ἑβδόματον δὲ
καὶ δέκατον ζητεῖν οὐκ ἐμόν, ἀλλὰ Διός.
εἰ δ᾽ ἐπὶ πρεσβυτέρους τις ἔχει πόθον, οὐκέτι παίζει,
ἀλλ᾽ ἤδη ζητεῖ "τὸν δ᾽ ἀπαμειβόμενος."

I   STRATO

"Begin with Zeus," Aratus said; but, Muse,
   I do not think I'll trouble you today.
If hanging out with boys is what I choose
   To do, does that concern you anyway?

II   STRATO

Don't look for pious Priam in these pages,
Niobe's tears, Medea's jealous rages,
Nor Itys and his nightingales—enough
My predecessors scribbled of such stuff!
But Love, surrounded by the simpering Graces,
And Bacchus are ill-suited to straight faces.

III   STRATO

Diodorus, boys' things come in three
Shapes and sizes; learn them handily:
      When unstripped it's a dick,
      But when stiff it's a prick:
Wanked, you know what its nickname must be.

IV   STRATO

A twelve-year-old looks fetching in his prime,
Thirteen's an even more beguiling time.
That lusty bloom blows sweeter at fourteen;
Sexier yet a boy just turned fifteen.
The sixteenth year seems perfectly divine,
And seventeen is Jove's tidbit, not mine.
But if you fall for older fellows, that
Suggests child's play no more but tit-for-tat.

4

V ΣΤΡΑΤΩΝΟΣ

Τοὺς λευκοὺς ἀγαπῶ, φιλέω δ᾽ ἅμα τοὺς μελιχρώδεις
καὶ ξανθούς, στέργω δ᾽ ἔμπαλι τοὺς μέλανας.
οὐδὲ κόρας ξανθὰς παραπέμπομαι· ἀλλὰ περισσῶς
τοὺς μελανοφθάλμους αἰγλοφανεῖς τε φιλῶ.

VI ΣΤΡΑΤΩΝΟΣ

Πρωκτὸς καὶ χρυσὸς τὴν αὐτὴν ψῆφον ἔχουσιν·
ψηφίζων δ᾽ ἀφελῶς τοῦτό ποθ᾽ εὗρον ἐγώ.

VII ΣΤΡΑΤΩΝΟΣ

Σφιγκτὴρ οὐκ ἔστιν παρὰ παρθένῳ, οὐδὲ φίλημα
ἁπλοῦν, οὐ φυσικὴ χρωτὸς ἐϋπνοΐη,
οὐ λόγος ἡδὺς ἐκεῖνος ὁ πορνικός, οὐδ᾽ ἀκέραιον
βλέμμα, διδασκομένη δ᾽ ἐστὶ κακιοτέρα.
ψυχροῦνται δ᾽ ὄπιθεν πᾶσαι· τὸ δὲ μεῖζον ἐκεῖνο,
οὐκ ἔστιν ποῦ θῇς τὴν χέρα πλαζομένην.

VIII ΣΤΡΑΤΩΝΟΣ

Εἶδον ἐγώ τινα παῖδα † ἐπανθοπλοκοῦντα κόρυμβον,
ἄρτι παρερχόμενος τὰ στεφανηπλόκια·
οὐδ᾽ ἄτρωτα παρῆλθον· ἐπιστὰς δ᾽ ἥσυχος αὐτῷ
φημὶ "Πόσου πωλεῖς τὸν σὸν ἐμοὶ στέφανον;"
μᾶλλον τῶν καλύκων δ᾽ ἐρυθαίνετο, καὶ κατακύψας
φησὶ "Μακρὰν χώρει, μή σε πατὴρ ἐσίδῃ."
ὠνοῦμαι προφάσει στεφάνους, καὶ οἴκαδ᾽ ἀπελθὼι·
ἐστεφάνωσα θεούς, κεῖνον ἐπευξάμενος.

IX ΣΤΡΑΤΩΝΟΣ

Ἄρτι καλός, Διόδωρε, σύ, καὶ φιλέουσι πέπειρος·
ἀλλὰ καὶ ἢν γήμῃς, οὐκ ἀπολειψόμεθα.

5

V STRATO

Pale skins I like, but honey-coloured more,
And blond and brunette boys I both adore.
I never blackball brown eyes, but above
All, eyes of scintillating black I love.

VI STRATO

That *ass* is the metrical equivalent
Of *cash* I discovered once by accident.

VII STRATO

Loose girls lose their grip. They wear cheap scent.
Their kisses aren't sincere or innocent.
Sweet smut is one thing they're no good at talking.
Their looks are sly. The worst is a bluestocking.
Moreover, fundamentally they're cold;
They've nothing for a groping hand to hold.

VIII STRATO

Remarking as I passed a flower-stall
    A lad entwining buds and blooms together,
Smitten, I paused to ask him in a small
    Voice how much his garland cost and whether
He'd sell it me? He hung his head and blushed
    Like a rose: "Go on! or Dad will take a dim
View . . . " I bought a token wreath and rushed
    Off home to bedeck and beseech the gods for him.

IX STRATO

Delicious Diodorus, ripe for bed,
We'll not forsake you even when you wed.

X   ΣΤΡΑΤΩΝΟΣ

Εἰ καί σοι τριχόφοιτος ἐπεσκίρτησεν ἴουλος,
καὶ τρυφεραὶ κροτάφων ξανθοφεῖς ἕλικες,
οὐδ᾿ οὕτω φεύγω τὸν ἐρώμενον· ἀλλὰ τὸ κάλλος
τούτου, κἂν πώγων, κἂν τρίχες, ἡμέτερον.

XI   ΣΤΡΑΤΩΝΟΣ

Ἐχθὲς ἔχων ἀνὰ νύκτα Φιλόστρατον, οὐκ ἐδυνήθην,
κείνου, πῶς εἴπω; πάντα παρασχομένου.
ἀλλ᾿ ἐμὲ μηκέτ᾿ ἔχοιτε φίλοι φίλον, ἀλλ᾿ ἀπὸ πύργου
ῥίψατ᾿, ἐπεὶ λίην Ἀστυάναξ γέγονα.

XII   ΦΛΑΚΚΟΥ

Ἄρτι γενειάζων ὁ καλὸς καὶ στερρὸς ἐρασταῖς
παιδὸς ἐρᾷ Λάδων. σύντομος ἡ Νέμεσις.

XIII   ΣΤΡΑΤΩΝΟΣ

Ἰητροὺς εὗρόν ποτ᾿ ἐγὼ λείους δυσέρωτας,
τρίβοντας φυσικῆς φάρμακον ἀντιδότου.
οἱ δέ γε φωραθέντες, "Ἔχ᾿ ἡσυχίην" ἐδέοντο·
κἀγὼ ἔφην "Σιγῶ, καὶ θεραπεύσετέ με."

XIV   ΔΙΟΣΚΟΡΙΔΟΥ

Δημόφιλος τοιοῖσδε φιλήμασιν εἰ πρὸς ἐραστὰς
χρήσεται ἀκμαίην, Κύπρι, καθ᾿ ἡλικίην,
ὡς ἐμὲ νῦν ἐφίλησεν ὁ νήπιος, οὐκέτι νύκτωρ
ἥσυχα τῇ κείνου μητρὶ μενεῖ πρόθυρα.

X   STRATO

Notwithstanding that hairs, as I feared,
On your temples have lately appeared,
    And your chin and your cheek,
    My beloved's physique
Is still mine, though he's growing a beard.

XI   STRATO

When I had Philostratus last night
He was tight and did everything right,
    But I couldn't get hard;
    Now my friends will discard
Me for not doing all Sodom might.

XII   FLACCUS

So fair, (but to his suitors so unfair),
Lado has barely grown some pubic hair
Yet loves a lad: what swift comeuppance there!

XIII   STRATO

I surprised once some hardy young chaps
Playing doctor, near to a relapse.
    When they begged me keep mum,
    I replied, "I'll play dumb,
If you're willing to treat me, perhaps."

XIV   DIOSCORIDES

If Deophilus, who was no more
Than a child when he kissed me before,
    As an adult should kiss
    His admirers like this,
They'll be beating a path to his door.

8

XV   ΣΤΡΑΤΩΝΟΣ

Εἰ Γραφικοῦ πυγαῖα σανὶς δέδαχ᾽ ἐν βαλανείῳ,
ἄνθρωπους τί πάθω; καὶ ξύλον αἰσθάνεται.

XVI   ΣΤΡΑΤΩΝΟΣ

Μὴ κρύπτης τὸν ἔρωτα, Φιλόκρατες· αὐτὸς ὁ δαίμων
λακτίζειν κραδίην ἡμετέρην ἱκανός·
ἀλλ᾽ ἱλαροῦ μετάδος τι φιλήματος. ἔσθ᾽ ὅτε καὶ σὺ
αἰτήσεις τοιάνδ᾽ ἐξ ἑτέρων χάριτα.

XVII   ΑΔΗΛΟΝ

Οὔ μοι θῆλυς ἔρως ἐγκάρδιος, ἀλλά με πυρσοὶ
ἄρσενες ἀσβέστῳ θῆκαν ὑπ᾽ ἀνθρακιῇ.
πλειότερον τόδε θάλπος· ὅσον δυνατώτερος ἄρσην
θηλυτέρης, τόσσον χὠ πόθος ὀξύτερος.

XVIII   ΑΛΦΕΙΟΥ ΜΙΤΥΛΗΝΑΙΟΥ

Τλήμονες, οἷς ἀνέραστος ἔφυ βίος· οὔτε γὰρ ἔρξαι
εὐμαρές, οὔτ᾽ εἰπεῖν ἐστί τι νόσφι πόθων.
καὶ γὰρ ἐγὼ νῦν εἰμὶ λίην βραδύς· εἰ δ᾽ ἐπίδοιμι
Ξεινόφιλον, στεροπῆς πτήσομαι ὀξύτερος.
τοὔνεκεν οὐ φεύγειν γλυκὺν ἵμερον, ἀλλὰ διώκειν
πᾶσι λέγω. ψυχῆς ἐστιν Ἔρως ἀκόνη.

XIX   ΑΔΗΛΟΝ

Οὐ δύναμαί σε θέλων θέσθαι φίλον· οὔτε γὰρ αἰτεῖς,
οὔτ᾽ αἰτοῦντι δίδως, οὔθ᾽ ἃ δίδωμι δέχῃ.

XV   STRATO

A board at the baths pinched Graphicus' ass, revealing
That even wood is capable of feeling.

XVI   STRATO

Don't be coy, Philostratus: divine
Love can trample on your heart and mine.
    Only kiss me today;
      You'll discover one day
Yours are favours that some may decline.

XVII   ANONYMOUS

The love of women leaves me cold; desire
For men, though, scorches me with coals of fire.
As women are the weaker sex, my yen
Is stronger, warmer, more intense for men.

XVIII   ALPHEIUS OF MYTILENE

A loveless life is hell, no doubt about
It; one can't say or do a thing without
Longing. If Xenophilus came in sight,
Slow though I am, I'd reach the speed of light.
Far from avoiding what you can't control,
Pursue it. Love's the whetstone of the soul.

XIX   ANONYMOUS

I can't befriend you, eager though I am:
    You ask for nothing, neither will you grant
    Me anything I ask for; adamant,
For all my gifts you do not give a damn.

XX   ΙΟΥΛΙΟΥ ΛΕΩΝΙΔΑ

Ὁ Ζεὺς Αἰθιόπων πάλι τέρπεται εἰλαπίναισιν,
ἢ χρυσὸς Δανάης εἴρπυσεν εἰς θαλάμους·
θαῦμα γὰρ εἰ Περίανδρον ἰδὼν οὐχ ἥρπασε γαίης
τὸν καλόν· ἢ φιλόπαις οὐκέτι νῦν ὁ θεός.

XXI   ΣΤΡΑΤΩΝΟΣ

Κλέψομεν ἄχρι τίνος τὰ φιλήματα, καὶ τὰ λαθραῖα
νεύσομεν ἀλλήλοις ὄμμασι φειδομένοις;
μέχρι τίνος δ᾽ ἀτέλεστα λαλήσομεν, ἀμβολίαισι
ζευγνύντες κενεὰς ἔμπαλιν ἀμβολίας;
μέλλοντες τὸ καλὸν δαπανήσομεν· ἀλλὰ πρὶν ἐλθεῖν
τὰς φθονεράς, Φείδων, θῶμεν ἐπ᾽ ἔργα λόγοις.

XXII   ΣΚΥΘΙ-ΟΥ

Ἦλθέν μοι μέγα πῆμα, μέγας πόλεμος, μέγα μοι πῦρ,
Ἤλισσος πλήρης τῶν ἐς ἔρωτ᾽ ἐτέων,
αὐτὰ τὰ καίρι᾽ ἔχων ἑκκαίδεκα, καὶ μετὰ τούτων
πάσας καὶ μικρὰς καὶ μεγάλας χάριτας,
καὶ πρὸς ἀναγνῶναι φωνὴν μέλι, καὶ τὸ φιλῆσαι
χείλεα, καὶ τὸ λαβεῖν ἔνδον, ἀμεμπτότατον.
καὶ τί πάθω; φησὶν γὰρ ὁρᾶν μόνον· ἦ ῥ᾽ ἀγρυπνήσω
πολλάκι, τῇ κενεῇ κύπριδι χειρομαχῶν.

XXIII   ΜΕΛΕΑΓΡΟΥ

Ἠγρεύθην ὁ πρόσθεν ἐγώ ποτε τοῖς δυσέρωσι
κώμοις ἠϊθέων πολλάκις ἐγγελάσας·
καί μ᾽ ἐπὶ σοῖς ὁ πτανὸς Ἔρως προθύροισι, Μυΐσκε,
στῆσεν ἐπιγράψας "Σκῦλ᾽ ἀπὸ Σωφροσύνης."

XX   JULIUS LEONIDAS

Is Zeus carousing with the blacks, I wonder,
  Or visiting Danaë disguised as gold,
That he has not picked up fair Periander—
  Or is he not the paederast of old?

XXI   STRATO

How long need we sneak kisses, with oblique
Glances at one another wink and peek?
How long chat in this inconclusive way,
Adding delay to meaningless delay?
Phido, let's waste no chance to work things out,
Before the killjoy hairs begin to sprout.

XXII   SCYTHINUS

Calamity and conflagration! Strife!
Elissus has attained the time of life,
Sixteen, that's made for love, and he has all
The adolescent graces great and small:
A honeyed voice, a mouth that's sweet to kiss,
And an accommodating orifice.
But, "Look, don't touch!" he tells me. What a fate!
I'll lie awake all night and—meditate.

XXIII   MELEAGER

I used to laugh at young men who were not
Successful in their wooing. Now I'm caught;
Myiscus, on your gate winged Love has placed
Me, labelled as, "A Trophy of the Chaste."

XXIV   ΛΑΥΡΕΑ

Εἴ μοι χαρτὸς ἐμὸς Πολέμων καὶ σῶος ἀνέλθοι,
οἷος α⟨.. Δήλου⟩ κοίρανε, πεμπόμενος,
ῥέξειν οὐκ ἀπόφημι τὸν ὀρθροβόην παρὰ βωμοῖς
ὄρνιν, ὃν εὐχωλαῖς ὡμολόγησα τεαῖς·
εἰ δέ τι τῶν ὄντων τότε οἱ πλέον ἢ καὶ ἔλασσον
ἔλθοι ἔχων, λέλυται τοὐμὸν ὑποσχέσιον.
ἦλθε δὲ σὺν πώγωνι. τόδ᾽ εἰ φίλον αὐτὸς ἑαυτῷ
εὔξατο, τὴν θυσίην πρᾶσσε τὸν εὐξάμενον.

XXV   ΣΤΑΤΥΛΛΙΟΥ ΦΛΑΚΚΟΥ

Σῶόν μοι Πολέμωνα μογεῖν, ὅτ᾽ ἔπεμπον, Ἀπόλλω
ἠτούμην, θυσίην ὄρνιν ὑποσχόμενος.
ἦλθε δέ μοι Πολέμων λάσιος γένυν. οὐ μὰ σέ, Φοῖβε,
ἦλθεν ἐμοί, πικρῷ δ᾽ ἐξέφυγέν με τάχει.
οὐκέτι σοι θύω τὸν ἀλέκτορα. μή με σοφίζου,
κωφήν μοι σταχύων ἀντιδιδοὺς καλάμην.

XXVI   ΣΤΑΤΥΛΛΙΟΥ ΦΛΑΚΚΟΥ

Εἴ μοι σωζόμενος Πολέμων ὃν ἔπεμπον ἀνέλθοι
⟨φοινίξειν βωμοὺς ὡμολόγησα τεούς⟩.
νῦν θ᾽ αὐτῷ Πολέμων ἀνασώζεται· οὐκέτ᾽ ἀφῖκται,
Φοῖβε, δασὺς δ᾽ ἥκων οὐκέτι σῶος ἐμοί.
αὐτὸς ἴσως σκιάσαι γένυν εὔξατο· θυέτω αὐτός,
ἀντία ταῖσιν ἐμαῖς ἐλπίσιν εὐξάμενος.

XXVII   ΣΤΑΤΥΛΛΙΟΥ ΦΛΑΚΚΟΥ

Σαῖς ἴκελον προὔπεμπον ἐγὼ Πολέμωνα παρειαῖς,
ἢν ἔλθῃ, θύσειν ὄρνιν ὑποσχόμενος·
οὐ δέχομαι φθονεροῖς, Παιάν, φρίσσοντα γενείοις,
τοιούτου τλήμων εἵνεκεν εὐξάμενος.

XXIV   TULLIUS LAUREAS

Should my Polemo come home safe to me
Just as he was when first he went to sea,
Phoebus, I'll not forget the cockerell
I promised you if everything went well.
If he returns with either more or less
Than he had then, my vows are meaningless.
He's come back with a beard! If that's the thing
He prayed for, let him make the offering!

XXV   STATYLLIUS FLACCUS

I promised you a cock, Apollo, when
Polemo came home safe to me again.
He came, but not to stay. His cheeks defaced
By fuzz, he fled from me with cruel haste.
No cock for you, Apollo! Would you cheat
Me with stubble in place of cream of wheat?

XXVI   STATYLLIUS FLACCUS

If my Polemo came back good as new,
Phoebus, I swore to sacrifice to you.
He's safe but not himself. Whiskers detract
A lot from his homecoming, that's a fact—
Whiskers he prayed for! Let him pay the price
Of my vain hopes, and make the sacrifice!

XXVII   STATYLLIUS FLACCUS

Seeing Polemo off smooth-cheeked as you,
    Phoebus, I pledged to get him back again
One cock. Poor me! he's not the boy I knew:
    His disobliging bristles I disdain.

οὐδὲ μάτην τίλλεσθαι ἀναίτιον ὄρνιν ἔοικεν,
ἢ συντιλλέσθω, Δήλιε, καὶ Πολέμων.

XXVIII ΝΟΥΜΗΝΙΟΥ ΤΑΡΣΕΩΣ

Κῦρος κύριός ἐστι· τί μοι μέλει, εἰ παρὰ γράμμα;
οὐκ ἀναγινώσκω τὸν καλόν, ἀλλὰ βλέπω.

XXIX ΑΛΚΑΙΟΥ

Πρώταρχος καλός ἐστι, καὶ οὐ θέλει· ἀλλὰ θελήσει
ὕστερον· ἡ δ᾽ ὥρη λαμπάδ᾽ ἔχουσα τρέχει.

XXX ΑΛΚΑΙΟΥ

Ἡ κνήμη, Νίκανδρε, δασύνεται· ἀλλὰ φύλαξαι,
μή σε καὶ ἡ πυγὴ ταὐτὸ παθοῦσα λάθῃ·
καὶ γνώσῃ φιλέοντος ὅση σπάνις. ἀλλ᾽ ἔτι καὶ νῦν
τῆς ἀμετακλήτου φρόντισον ἡλικίης.

XXXI ΦΑΝΙΟΥ

Ναὶ Θέμιν, ἀκρήτου καὶ τὸ σκύφος ᾧ σεσάλευμαι,
Πάμφιλε, βαιὸς ἔχει τὸν σὸν ἔρωτα χρόνος·
ἤδη γὰρ καὶ μηρὸς ὑπὸ τρίχα, καὶ γένυς ἡβᾷ,
καὶ Πόθος εἰς ἑτέρην λοιπὸν ἄγει μανίην.
ἀλλ᾽ ὅτε ⟨σοι⟩ σπινθῆρος ἔτ᾽ ἴχνια βαιὰ λέλειπται,
φειδωλὴν ἀπόθου· Καιρὸς Ἔρωτι φίλος.

XXXII ΘΥΜΟΚΛΕΟΥΣ

Μέμνῃ που, μέμνῃ, ὅτε τοι ἔπος ἱερὸν εἶπον·
Ὥρη κάλλιστον, χ᾽ ὥρη ἐλαφρότατον·
ὥρην οὐδ᾽ ὁ τάχιστος ἐν αἰθέρι παρφθάσει ὄρνις.
νῦν ἴδε, πάντ᾽ ἐπὶ γῆς ἄνθεα σεῦ κέχυται.

Why pluck that inoffensive bird in vain?
While you are at it, pluck Polemo too!

XXVIII   NUMENIUS OF TARSUS

Cyrus is serious, no open book—
But what do I care as long as I can look?

XXIX   ALCAEUS

Protarchus won't say Yes, but later on
He will—once all the fires of youth are gone.

XXX   ALCAEUS

Your legs, Nicander, are becoming hairy;
  Take care this doesn't happen to your ass,
Or you will find your lovers getting very
  Scarce. Irrevocably, your youth will pass.

XXXI   PHANIAS

By Themis, and this wine which makes me drunk,
Pamphilus, I think your lease on love has shrunk.
Hair on your thighs and on your cheeks suggests
Burgeoning heterosexual interests.
But if there's one spark left, don't be a tease!
Love overlooks no opportunities.

XXXII   THYMOCLES

"Loveliest," —remember when I made
  That hackneyed observation?—"is the spring,
But swifter than a bird upon the wing."
  Now see how fast your bloom begins to fade.

16

XXXIII ΜΕΛΕΑΓΡΟΥ
Ἦν καλὸς Ἡράκλειτος, ὅτ᾽ ἦν ποτέ· νῦν δὲ παρ᾽ ἥβην
κηρύσσει πόλεμον δέρρις ὀπισθοβάταις.
ἀλλά, Πολυξενίδη, τάδ᾽ ὁρῶν, μὴ γαῦρα φρυάσσου·
ἔστι καὶ ἐν γλουτοῖς φυομένη Νέμεσις.

XXXIV ΑΥΤΟΜΕΔΟΝΤΟΣ
Πρὸς τὸν παιδοτρίβην Δημήτριον ἐχθὲς ἐδείπνουν,
πάντων ἀνθρώπων τὸν μακαριστότατον.
εἷς αὐτοῦ κατέκειθ᾽ ὑποκόλπιος, εἷς ὑπὲρ ὦμον,
εἷς ἔφερεν τὸ φαγεῖν, εἷς δὲ πιεῖν ἐδίδου·
ἡ τετρὰς ἡ περίβλεπτος. ἐγὼ παίζων δὲ πρὸς αὐτὸν
φημὶ "Σὺ καὶ νύκτωρ, φίλτατε, παιδοτριβεῖς;"

XXXV ΔΙΟΚΛΕΟΥΣ
Χαῖρέ ποτ᾽ οὐκ εἰπόντα προσεῖπε τις· "Ἀλλ᾽ ὁ περισσὸς
κάλλεϊ νῦν Δάμων οὐδὲ τὸ χαῖρε λέγει.
ἥξει τις τούτου χρόνος ἔκδικος· εἶτα δασυνθεὶς
ἄρξῃ χαῖρε λέγειν οὐκ ἀποκρινομένοις."

XXXVI ΑΣΚΛΗΠΙΑΔΟΥ ΑΔΡΑΜΥΤΤΗΝΟΥ
Νῦν αἰτεῖς, ὅτε λεπτὸς ὑπὸ κροτάφοισιν ἴουλος
ἕρπει καὶ μηροῖς ὀξὺς ἔπεστι χνόος·
εἶτα λέγεις "Ἥδιον ἐμοὶ τόδε." καὶ τίς ἂν εἴποι
κρείσσονας αὐχμηρὰς ἀσταχύων καλάμας;

XXXVII ΔΙΟΣΚΟΡΙΔΟΥ
Πυγὴν Σωσάρχοιο διέπλασεν Ἀμφιπολίτεω
μυελίνην παίζων ὁ βροτολοιγὸς Ἔρως,
Ζῆνα θέλων ἐρεθίξαι, ὁθούνεκα τῶν Γανυμήδους
μηρῶν οἱ τούτου πουλὺ μελιχρότεροι.

XXXIII   MELEAGER

A peach was Heraclitus when—don't scoff!—
   Still Heraclitus; now he's past his prime
His hairy hide puts all assailants off.
   On your cheeks too the curse will come in time.

XXXIV   AUTOMEDON

I dined with coach Demetrius yesterday,
The luckiest of men! While one lad lay
Upon his lap, one by his shoulder stood;
One poured the drinks, another served the food.
I joked, "This foursome is a pretty sight!
And do you also coach the boys at night?"

XXXV   DIOCLES

Somebody said when snubbed, "Is Damon so
Beautiful he doesn't say hello?
Time will exact revenge when, bye and bye,
Grown hairy, he greets men who won't reply."

XXXVI   ASCLEPIADES OF ADRAMYTTIUM

Now you put out, when prickly down appears
Between your legs and underneath your ears.
"That feels so good!" you cry, "Do that again!"
But who prefers dry stubble to whole grain?

XXXVII   DIOSCORIDES

Cupid, who loves mankind to tantalize,
   Sculpted Sotarchus' bum for fun in butter,
   Provoking Zeus: those buns looked better
Than even Ganymede's ambrosial thighs.

18

XXXVIII   PIANOY

Ὡραί σοι Χάριτές τε κατὰ γλυκὺ χεῦαν ἔλαιον,
ὦ πυγά· κνώσσειν δ᾽ οὐδὲ γέροντας ἐᾷς.
λέξον μοι τίνος ἐσσὶ μάκαιρα τύ, καὶ τίνα παίδων
κοσμεῖς; ἁ πυγὰ δ᾽ εἶπε· "Μενεκράτεος."

XXXIX   ΛΔΗΛΟΝ

Ἐσβέσθη Νίκανδρος, ἀπέπτατο πᾶν ἀπὸ χροιῆς
ἄνθος, καὶ χαρίτων λοιπὸν ἔτ᾽ οὐδ᾽ ὄνομα,
ὃν πρὶν ἐν ἀθανάτοις ἐνομίζομεν. ἀλλὰ φρονεῖτε
μηδὲν ὑπὲρ θνητούς, ὦ νέοι· εἰσὶ τρίχες.

XL   ΑΔΗΛΟΝ

Μὴ 'κδύσῃς, ἄνθρωπε, τὸ χλαίνιον, ἀλλὰ θεώρει
οὕτως ἀκρολίθου κἀμὲ τρόπον ξοάνου.
γυμνὴν Ἀντιφίλου ζητῶν χάριν, ὡς ἐπ᾽ ἀκάνθαις
εὑρήσεις ῥοδέαν φυομένην κάλυκα.

XLI   ΜΕΛΕΑΓΡΟΥ

Οὐκέτι μοι Θήρων γράφεται καλός, οὐδ᾽ ὁ πυραυγὴς
πρίν ποτε, νῦν δ᾽ ἤδη δαλός, Ἀπολλόδοτος.
στέργω θῆλυν ἔρωτα· δασυτρώγλων δὲ πίεσμα
λασταύρων μελέτω ποιμέσιν αἰγοβάταις.

XLII   ΔΙΟΣΚΟΡΙΔΟΥ

Βλέψον ἐς Ἑρμογένην πλήρει χερί, καὶ τάχα πρήξεις
παιδοκόραξ ὧν σοι θυμὸς ὀνειροπολεῖ,
καὶ στυγνὴν ὀφρύων λύσεις τάσιν· ἢν δ᾽ ἁλιεύῃ
ὀρφανὸν ἀγκίστρου κύματι δοὺς κάλαμον,
ἕλξεις ἐκ λιμένος πολλὴν δρόσον· οὐδὲ γὰρ αἰδὼς
οὐδ᾽ ἔλεος δαπάνῳ κόλλοπι συντρέφεται.

XXXVIII   RHIANUS

Oh, what an ass! so gracefully lubricious
  You never even leave old men in peace.
Tell me, what boy do you adorn, delicious
  Bottom? The ass replied, "Menecrates."

XXXIX   ANONYMOUS

Nicander's finished, there is not a trace
Of bloom or loveliness left in a face
I called divine. So, mortal youths, beware
Immortal thoughts; remember pubic hair.

XL   ANONYMOUS

Don't take my clothes off! View me as a kind
  Of statue, draped so almost nothing shows.
If you look for my naked charms, you'll find
  Amid a scratchy bush my rosebud grows.

XLI   MELEAGER

No, Theron's beauty does no longer please
  Me, nor Apollodotus' burnt-out charms.
I like cunt. Let bestial goatherds squeeze
  Their hairy little bumboys in their arms!

XLII   DIOSCORDES

Do not go empty-handed if you look
  To win your heart's desire, Hermogenes,
And smile again. Be sure to bait your hook
  Well, or you will catch nothing. Qualities
Like shame and pity are, poor chickenhawk,
  Not natural to such a greedy tease.

20

XLIII ΚΑΛΛΙΜΑΧΟΥ

Ἐθαίρω τὸ ποίημα τὸ κυκλικόν, οὐδὲ κελεύθῳ
χαίρω τις πολλοὺς ὧδε καὶ ὧδε φέρει·
μισῶ καὶ περίφοιτον ἐρώμενον, οὐδ᾽ ἀπὸ κρήνης
πίνω· σικχαίνω πάντα τὰ δημόσια.
Λυσανίη, σὺ δὲ ναίχι καλὸς καλός· ἀλλὰ πρὶν εἰπεῖν
τοῦτο σαφῶς, ἠχὼ φησί τις "Ἄλλος ἔχει."

XLIV ΓΛΑΥΚΟΥ

Ἦν ὅτε παῖδας ἔπειθε πάλαι ποτὲ δῶρα φιλεῦντας
ὄρτυξ, καὶ ῥαπτὴ σφαῖρα, καὶ ἀστράγαλοι·
νῦν δὲ λοπὰς καὶ κέρμα· τὰ παίγνια δ᾽ οὐδὲν ἐκεῖνα
ἰσχύει. ζητεῖτ᾽ ἄλλο τι, παιδοφίλαι.

XLV ΠΟΣΕΙΔΙΠΠΟΥ

Ναὶ ναὶ βάλλετ᾽, Ἔρωτες· ἐγὼ σκοπὸς εἷς ἅμα πολλοῖς
κεῖμαι. μὴ φείσησθ᾽, ἄφρονες· ἢν γὰρ ἐμὲ
νικήσητ᾽, ὀνομαστοὶ ἐν ἀθανάτοισιν ἔσεσθε
τοξόται, ὡς μεγάλης δεσπόται ἰοδόκης.

XLVI ΑΣΚΛΗΠΙΑΔΟΥ

Οὐκ εἴμ᾽ οὐδ᾽ ἐτέων δύο κείκοσι, καὶ κοπιῶ ζῶν
Ὦρωτες, τι κακὸν τοῦτο; τί με φλέγετε;
ἢν γὰρ ἐγώ τι πάθω, τί ποιήσετε; δῆλον, Ἔρωτες,
ὡς τὸ πάρος παίξεσθ᾽ ἄφρονες ἀστραγάλοις.

XLVII ΜΕΛΕΑΓΡΟΥ

Ματρὸς ἔτ᾽ ἐν κόλποισιν ὁ νήπιος ὀρθρινὰ παίζων
ἀστραγάλοις τοὐμὸν πνεῦμ᾽ ἐκύβευσεν Ἔρως.

XLIII   CALLIMACHUS

Little I care for your popular cyclical poem:
    Such thoroughfares I thoroughly despise.
So I detest a boy who makes himself common,
    Nor do I drink from public water supplies.
Yes, you are handsome, Lysanias, terribly handsome.
    "*And* someone else's!" instantly Echo replies.

XLIV   GLAUCUS

Where once you could win over grasping boys
    With birds and balls and jacks, all that beguiles
Them now is sweets or cash; old-fashioned toys
    Don't work. Find something new, you pedophiles!

XLV   POSIDIPUS

Let fly, young Loves! I stand, the single butt
    Of all you brats. Don't spare me! Your success
Will win you fame, not just as marksmen, but
    For the impressive weapons you possess.

XLVI   ASCLEPIADES

Not twenty-two, yet I find life a stiff
    Proposition. Why such hard attacks,
You dizzy darlings? What would you do if
    I got hurt? Continue playing jacks?

XLVII   MELEAGER

An infant on his mother's lap Love lay
And in one morning diced my life away.

22

XLVIII   ΜΕΛΕΑΓΡΟΥ

Κεῖμαι· λὰξ ἐπίβαινε κατ᾽ αὐχένος, ἄγριε δαῖμον.
οἰδά σε, ναὶ μὰ θεούς, καὶ βαρὺν ὄντα φέρειν·
οἰδα καὶ ἔμπυρα τόξα. βαλὼν δ᾽ ἐπ᾽ ἐμὴν φρένα πυρσούς,
οὐ φλέξεις· ἤδη πᾶσα γάρ ἐστι τέφρη.

XLIX   ΜΕΛΕΑΓΡΟΥ

Ζωροπότει, δύσερως, καὶ σοῦ φλόγα τὰν φιλόπαιδα
κοιμάσει λάθας δωροδότας Βρόμιος·
ζωροπότει, καὶ πλῆρες ἀφυσσάμενος σκύφος οἴνας,
ἔκκρουσον στυγερὰν ἐκ κραδίας ὀδύναν.

L   ΑΣΚΛΗΠΙΑΔΟΥ

Πῖν᾽, Ἀσκληπιάδη· τί τὰ δάκρυα ταῦτα; τί πάσχεις;
οὐ σὲ μόνον χαλεπὴ Κύπρις ἐληΐσατο,
οὐδ᾽ ἐπὶ σοὶ μούνῳ κατεθήξατο τόξα καὶ ἰοὺς
πικρὸς Ἔρως. τί ζῶν ἐν σποδιῇ τίθεσαι;
πίνωμεν Βάκχου ζωρὸν πόμα· δάκτυλος ἀώς·
ἦ πάλι κοιμιστὰν λύχνον ἰδεῖν μένομεν;
πίνομεν οὐ γὰρ ἔρως· μετά τοι χρόνον οὐκέτι πουλύν,
σχέτλιε, τὴν μακρὰν νύκτ᾽ ἀναπαυσόμεθα.

LI   ΚΑΛΛΙΜΑΧΟΥ

Ἔγχει, καὶ πάλιν εἰπέ, Διοκλέος· οὐδ᾽ Ἀχελῷος
κείνου τῶν ἱερῶν αἰσθάνεται κυάθων.
καλὸς ὁ παῖς, Ἀχελῷε, λίην καλός· εἰ δέ τις οὐχι
φησὶν—ἐπισταίμην μοῦνος ἐγὼ τὰ καλά.

LII   ΜΕΛΕΑΓΡΟΥ

Οὔριος ἐμπνεύσας ναύταις Νότος, ὦ δυσέρωτες,
ἤμισύ μευ ψυχᾶς ἄρπασεν Ἀνδράγαθον.

XLVIII   MELEAGER

Yes, kick me when I'm down, you spiteful sprite!
  I feel your weight, I feel your fiery dart.
  But if you try to set fire to my heart,
You can't: it is incinerated quite.

XLIX   MELEAGER

Drink deep, boy-lover. Bacchus, bringer of
Oblivion, will soothe your hopeless love.
Drink deep, and as you drain the wine-filled bowl
Purge all the bitter anguish from your soul.

L   ASCLEPIADES

What's wrong, Asclepiades? Drink, don't weep!
Not you alone does cruel Venus keep
In thrall; not you alone is pungent lust
Transfixing. Why lie panting in the dust?
Drink unmixed wine. The east's just touched with red;
Let's wait for its lamp to light our way to bed
Once more. Poor, lovelorn wretch, drink deep:
Short is the time before our long, long sleep.

LI   CALLIMACHUS

Drinking to Diocles, don't dilute
  The toast that I propose to honour his
Beauty: and if you call that in dispute,
  I'll be the one to say what beauty is!

LII   MELEAGER

Borne on a fair south wind, Andragathon
Has sailed away, and half my soul is gone.

24

τρὶς μάκαρες νᾶες, τρὶς δ᾽ ὄλβια κύματα πόντου,
τετράκι δ᾽ εὐδαίμων παιδοφορῶν ἄνεμος.
εἴθ᾽ εἴην δελφίς, ἵν᾽ ἐμοῖς βαστακτὸς ἐπ᾽ ὤμοις
πορθμευθεὶς ἐσίδῃ τὰν γλυκόπαιδα Ῥόδον.

LIII   ΜΕΛΕΑΓΡΟΥ

Εὔφορτοι νᾶες πελαγίτιδες, αἳ πόρον Ἕλλης
πλεῖτε, καλὸν κόλποις δεξάμεναι Βορέην,
ἤν που ἐπ᾽ ἠϊόνων Κώαν κατὰ νᾶσον ἴδητε
Φανίον εἰς χαροπὸν δερκομέναν πέλαγος,
τοῦτ᾽ ἔπος ἀγγείλαιτε, καλαὶ νέες, ὥς με κομίζει
ἵμερος οὐ ναύταν, ποσσὶ δὲ πεζοπόρον.
εἰ γὰρ τοῦτ᾽ εἴποιτ᾽, εὖ τέλοι, αὐτίκα καὶ Ζεὺς
οὔριος ὑμετέρας πνεύσεται εἰς ὀθόνας.

LIV   ΜΕΛΕΑΓΡΟΥ

Ἀρνεῖται τὸν Ἔρωτα τεκεῖν ἡ Κύπρις, ἰδοῦσα
ἄλλον ἐν ἠϊθέοις Ἵμερον Ἀντίοχον.
ἀλλά, νέοι, στέργοιτε νέον Πόθον· ἦ γὰρ ὁ κοῦρος
εὕρηται κρείσσων οὗτος Ἔρωτος Ἔρως.

LV   ΑΔΗΛΟΝ, οἱ δὲ ΑΡΤΕΜΩΝΟΣ

Λητοΐδη, σὺ μὲν ἔσχες ἁλίρρυτον αὐχένα Δήλου,
κοῦρε Διὸς μεγάλου, θέσφατα πᾶσι λέγων·
Κεκροπίαν δ᾽ Ἐχέδημος, ὁ δεύτερος Ἀτθίδι Φοῖβος,
ᾧ καλὸν ἁβροκόμης ἄνθος ἔλαμψεν Ἔρως.
ἡ δ᾽ ἀνὰ κῦμ᾽ ἄρξασα καὶ ἐν χθονὶ πατρὶς Ἀθήνη
νῦν κάλλει δούλην Ἑλλάδ᾽ ὑπηγάγετο.

LVI   ΜΕΛΕΑΓΡΟΥ

Εἰκόνα μὲν Παρίην ζωογλύφος ἄνυσ᾽ Ἔρωτος
Πραξιτέλης, Κύπριδος παῖδα τυπωσάμενος,

Blessed the ships, the waves themselves are glad,
And fortunate the wind that blows the lad.
I wish I were a dolphin, so astride
My back to Rhodes, sweet boys' home, he could ride.

LIII   MELEAGER

Sea-faring freighters, the next time you sail
The Hellespont with a mild Northern gale,
If on the beach of Cos you chance to see
Phanion gazing at the grey-blue sea,
Say that desire is bringing me there, and
Not by sea, fair ships, but overland,
And straightaway a god-sent wind will blow
And fill your sails, if you will tell her so.

LIV   MELEAGER

Venus, denying Cupid is her son,
Finds in Antiochus a better one.
This is the boy to be enamoured of,
Boys, a new love superior to Love.

LV   ARTEMON?

Hail, son of Zeus and Leto! Where the seas
Wash Delos you dispense your prophecies.
Your counterpart is Echedemus, whom
Love has illumined with bewitching bloom,
So Athens, mistress of the land and sea
By beauty holds all Greece in slavery.

LVI   MELEAGER

Praxiteles once carved a statue of
Venus' son, the pretty god of love,

νῦν δ᾽ ὁ θεῶν κάλλιστος Ἔρως ἔμψυχον ἄγαλμα,
αὐτὸν ἀπεικονίσας, ἔπλασε Πραξιτέλην·
ὄφρ᾽ ὁ μὲν ἐν θνατοῖς, ὁ δ᾽ ἐν αἰθέρι φίλτρα βραβεύῃ,
γῆς θ᾽ ἅμα καὶ μακάρων σκηπτροφορῶσι πόθοι.
ὀλβίστη Μερόπων ἱερὰ πόλις, ἃ θεόπαιδα
καινὸν Ἔρωτα νέων θοέψεν ὑφαγεμόνα.

LVII   ΜΕΛΕΑΓΡΟΥ

Πραξιτέλης ὁ πάλαι ζωογλύφος ἁβρὸν ἄγαλμα
ἄψυχον, μορφᾶς κωφὸν ἔτευξε τύπον,
πέτρον ἐνειδοφορῶν· ὁ δὲ νῦν, ἔμψυχα μαγεύων,
τὸν τριπανοῦργον Ἔρωτ᾽ ἔπλασεν ἐν κραδίᾳ.
ἦ τάχα τοὔνομ᾽ ἔχει ταὐτὸν μόνον, ἔργα δὲ κρέσσω,
οὐ λίθον, ἀλλὰ φρενῶν πνεῦμα μεταρρυθμίσας.
ἵλαος πλάσσοι τὸν ἐμὸν τρόπον, ὄφρα τυπώσας
ἐντὸς ἐμὴν ψυχὴν ναὸν Ἔρωτος ἔχῃ.

LVIII   ΡΙΑΝΟΥ

Ἡ Τροιζὴν ἀγαθὴ κουροτρόφος· οὐκ ἂν ἁμάρτοις
αἰνήσας παίδων οὐδὲ τὸν ὑστάτιον.
τόσσον δ᾽ Ἐμπεδοκλῆς φανερώτερος, ὅσσον ἐν ἄλλοις
ἄνθεσιν εἰαρινοῖς καλὸν ἔλαμψε ῥόδον.

LIX   ΜΕΛΕΑΓΡΟΥ

Ἁβρούς, ναὶ τὸν Ἔρωτα, τρέφει Τύρος· ἀλλὰ Μυΐσκος
ἔσβεσεν ἐκλάμψας ἀστέρας ἠέλιος.

LX   ΜΕΛΕΑΓΡΟΥ

Ἢν ἐνίδω Θήρωνα, τὰ πάνθ᾽ ὁρῶ· ἢν δὲ τὰ πάντα
βλέψω, τόνδε δὲ μή, τἄμπαλιν οὐδὲν ὁρῶ.

Who in his lovely image modelled this
Praxiteles, a living masterpiece,
So one on earth and one in heaven might reign,
Two Loves to deal love-charms to gods and men.
Blest isle of Cos for rearing this new-sprung
God-given Love, ring-leader of the young!

LVII   MELEAGER

Praxiteles once from marble sculpted some
Image of beauty, lifeless, stony, dumb.
His modern namesake, by his magic art,
Modelled Love's lively likeness in my heart.
The name's the same; his works are more refined:
Instead of marble he transforms the mind.
I wish that he would kindly mould my whole
Nature and build Love's temple in my soul.

LVIII   RHIANUS

Troezen grows sweet boys; you would not err
In praising the most unprepossessing there.
Empedocles with as much more splendour glows,
As does amid spring flowers the gorgeous rose.

LIX   MELEAGER

Love, Tyre breeds pretty boys, but as the sun
The stars, Myiscus outshines every one.

LX   MELEAGER

When I see Thero I see everything;
But when he's absent I can't see a thing.

LXI   ΑΔΗΛΟΝ

Ἄθρει· μὴ διὰ παντὸς ὅλαν κατάτηκ᾽, Ἀρίβαζε,
τὰν Κνίδον· ἁ πέτρα θρυπτομένα φέρεται.

LXII   ΑΛΛΟ

Ματέρες αἱ Περσῶν, καλὰ μὲν καλὰ τέκνα τεκεσθε·
ἀλλ᾽ Ἀρίβαζος ἐμοὶ κάλλιον ἢ τὸ καλόν.

LXIII   ΜΕΛΕΑΓΡΟΥ

Σιγῶν Ἡράκλειτος ἐν ὄμμασι τοῦτ᾽ ἔπος αὐδᾷ·
"Καὶ Ζηνὸς φλέξω πῦρ τὸ κεραυνοβόλον."
ναὶ μὴν καὶ Διόδωρος ἐνὶ στέρνοις τόδε φωνεῖ·
"Καὶ πέτρον τήκω χρωτὶ χλιαινόμενον."
δύστανος, παίδων ὃς ἐδέξατο τοῦ μὲν ἀπ᾽ ὄσσων
λαμπάδα, τοῦ δὲ πόθοις τυφόμενον γλυκὺ πῦρ.

LXIV   ΑΛΚΑΙΟΥ

Ζεὺς Πίσης μεδέων, Πειθήνορα, δεύτερον υἷα
Κύπριδος, αἰπεινῷ στέψον ὑπὸ Κρονίῳ·
μηδέ μοι οἰνοχόον κυλίκων σέθεν αἰετὸς ἀρθεὶς
μάρψαις ἀντὶ καλοῦ, κοίρανε, Δαρδανίδου.
εἰ δέ τι Μουσάων τοι ἐγὼ φίλον ὤπασα δῶρον,
νεύσαις μοι θείου παιδὸς ὁμοφροσύνην.

LXV   ΜΕΛΕΑΓΡΟΥ

Εἰ Ζεὺς κεῖνος ἔτ᾽ ἐστίν, ὁ καὶ Γανυμήδεος ἀκμὴν
ἁρπάξας, ἵν᾽ ἔχῃ νέκταρος οἰνοχόον,
κἠμοὶ τὸν καλόν ἐστιν ⟨ἐρὶ⟩ σπλάγχνοισι Μυΐσκον
κρύπτειν, μή με λάθῃ παιδὶ βαλὼν πτέρυγας.

LXI   ANONYMOUS

Watch out, Aribazus! Don't seduce
All Cnidus! The very stones are coming loose.

LXII   ANONYMOUS

You Persian mothers, what fair boys you bear!
But mine to me seems something more than fair.

LXIII   MELEAGER

Dumb Heraclitus signals with his eyes,
"I can ignite the lightning from the skies!"
And Diodorus secretly repeats,
"I melt the stone my body overheats."
Poor sod, who from the eyes of one takes fire
And scents the other's smouldering desire!

LXIV   ALCAEUS

Zeus, lord of Pisa, crown another son
    Of Cypris, Peithenor, born to succeed.
Like an eagle pray don't grab this one
    To pour your drinks instead of Ganymede.
Join me and the godlike boy in unison
    If I brought you poetic gifts indeed.

LXV   MELEAGER

Is Zeus the same who kidnapped Ganymede
    To have his nectar beautifully served?
Pretty Myiscus privately I need
    To keep, lest Zeus swoop on him unobserved.

LXVI   ΑΔΗΛΟΝ

Κρίνατ᾽, Ἔρωτες, ὁ παῖς τίνος ἄξιος. εἰ μὲν ἀληθῶς
ἀθανάτων, ἐχέτω· Ζανὶ γὰρ οὐ μάχομαι.
εἰ δέ τι καὶ θνατοῖς ὑπολείπεται, εἴπατ᾽, Ἔρωτες,
Δωρόθεος τίνος ἦν, καὶ τίνι νῦν δέδοται.
ἐν φανερῷ φωνεῦσιν· ἐμὴ χάρις.—ἀλλ᾽ ἀποχωρεῖ.
μὴ μετι πρὸς τὸ καλὸν καὶ σὺ μάταια φέρῃ.

LXVII   ΑΔΗΛΟΝ

Τὸν καλὸν οὐχ ὁρόω Διονύσιον. ἆρά γ᾽ ἀναρθείς,
Ζεῦ πάτερ, ⟨ἀθανάτοις⟩ δεύτερος οἰνοχοεῖ;
αἰετέ, τὸν χαρίεντα, ποτὶ πτερὰ πυκνὰ τινάξας,
πῶς ἔφερες; μή που κνίσματ᾽ ὄνυξιν ἔχει;

LXVIII   ΜΕΛΕΑΓΡΟΥ

Οὐκ ἐθέλω Χαρίδαμον· ὁ γὰρ καλὸς εἰς Δία λεύσσει,
ὡς ἤδη νέκταρ τῷ θεῷ οἰνοχοῶν·
οὐκ ἐθέλω· τί δέ μοι τὸν ἐπουρανιων βασιλῆα
ἄνταθλον νίκης τῆς ἐν ἔρωτι λαβεῖν;
ἀρκοῦμαι δ᾽, ἢν μοῦνον ὁ παῖς ἀνιὼν ἐς Ὄλυμπον,
ἐκ γῆς νίπτρα ποδῶν δάκρυα τἀμὰ λάβῃ,
μναμόσυνον στοργῆς· γλυκὺ δ᾽ ὄμμασι νεῦμα δίυγρον
δοίη, καί τι φίλημ᾽ ἁρπάσαι ἀκροθιγές.
τἄλλα δὲ πάντ᾽ ἐχέτω Ζεύς, ὡς θέμις· εἰ δ᾽ ἐθελήσοι,
ἦ τάχα που κἠγὼ γεύσομαι ἀμβροσίας.

LXIX   ΑΔΗΛΟΝ

Ζεῦ, προτέρῳ τέρπου Γανυμήδεϊ· τὸν δ᾽ ἐμόν, ὦναξ,
Δέξανδρον δέρκευ τηλόθεν· οὐ φθονέω.
εἰ δὲ βίῃ τὸν καλὸν ἀποίσεαι, οὐκέτ᾽ ἀνεκτῶς
δεσπόζεις· ἀπίτω καὶ τὸ βιοῦν ἐπὶ σοῦ.

LXVI   ANONYMOUS

Who does this boy deserve? Let Love decide!
    If fit for the gods, I do not strive with heaven;
Should anything for mortal men abide,
    Whose was he then? to whom is he now given?
I won, but Dorotheus took his leave.
Don't be the next one whom good looks deceive!

LXVII   ANONYMOUS

I don't see pretty Dionysius—
    Zeus, for a new pot-boy did you snatch him?
When with swift wings you bore the beauteous
    Lad off, I hope your talons did not scratch him!

LXVIII   MELEAGER

I don't want Charidamus. He looks up
To Zeus as if indeed he were his cup-
Bearer. Why take the king of heaven for
Successful sexual competitor?
Sufficient if, Olympus-bound, my sweet
With my terrestrial tears will wash his feet
In memory of my love—and add to this
One melting glance, one superficial kiss.
Let Zeus have all the rest. Should he allow,
I too shall taste ambrosia, somehow.

LXIX   ANONYMOUS

Take pleasure, Zeus, in your first catamite
    And gaze from afar at mine. I am forgiving.
But if you carry off the boy by might
    Your tyranny will make life not worth living.

32

LXX ΜΕΛΕΑΓΡΟΥ

Στήσομ' ἐγὼ καὶ Ζηνὸς ἐναντίον, εἴ σε, Μυΐσκε,
ἁρπάζειν ἐθέλοι νέκταρος οἰνοχόον.
καίτοι πολλάκις αὐτὸς ἐμοὶ τάδ' ἔλεξε· "Τί ταρβεῖς;
"οὔ σε βαλῶ ζήλοις· οἶδα παθὼν ἐλεεῖν."
χὠ μὲν δὴ τάδε φησίν· ἐγὼ δ', ἢν μυῖα παραπτῇ,
ταρβῶ μὴ ψεύστης Ζεὺς ἐπ' ἐμοὶ γέγονεν.

LXXI ΚΑΛΛΙΜΑΧΟΥ

Θεσσαλικὲ Κλεόνικε τάλαν, τάλαν· οὐ μὰ τὸν ὀξὺν
ἥλιον, οὐκ ἔγνων· σχέτλιε, ποῦ γέγονας;
ὀστέα σοι καὶ μοῦνον ἔτι τρίχες. ἦ ῥά σε δαίμων
οὑμὸς ἔχει, χαλεπῇ δ' ἤντεο θευμορίῃ;
ἔγνων· Εὐξίθεός σε συνήρπασε· καὶ σὺ γὰρ ἐλθὼν
τὸν καλόν, ὠμοχθήρ', ἔβλεπες ἀμφοτέροις.

LXXII ΜΕΛΕΑΓΡΟΥ

Ἤδη μὲν γλυκὺς ὄρθρος· ὁ δ' ἐν προθύροισιν ἄϋπνος
Δᾶμις ἀποψύχει πνεῦμα τὸ λειφθὲν ἔτι,
σχέτλιος, Ἡράκλειτον ἰδών· ἔστη γὰρ ὑπ' αὐγὰς
ὀφθαλμῶν, βληθεὶς κηρὸς ἐς ἀνθρακιήν.
ἀλλά μοι ἔγρεο, Δᾶμι δυσάμμορε· καὐτὸς Ἔρωτος
ἕλκος ἔχων ἐπὶ σοῖς δάκρυσι δακρυχέω.

LXXIII ΚΑΛΛΙΜΑΧΟΥ

Ἥμισύ μευ ψυχῆς ἔτι τὸ πνέον, ἥμισυ δ' οὐκ οἶδ'
εἴτ' Ἔρος εἴτ' Ἀΐδης ἥρπασε· πλὴν ἀφανές.
ἦ ῥά τιν' ἐς παίδων πάλιν ᾤχετο; καὶ μὲν ἀπεῖπον
πολλάκι· "Τὴν δρῆστιν μὴ ὑποδέχεσθε, νέοι."
†ουκισυ δίφησου· ἐκεῖσε γὰρ ἡ λιθόλευστος
κείνη καὶ δύσερως οἶδ' ὅτι που στρέφεται.

LXX   MELEAGER

I shall stand up to Zeus, should he design
To snap Myiscus up to serve his wine.
Zeus often said to me himself, "Afraid
I'll make you jealous? Sympathy has made
Me merciful." The antics of this fly *
Alarm me: can an eagle tell a lie?

LXXI   CALLIMACHUS

Cleonicus, poor sod, where have you been?
I'd hardly recognize you, sight unseen,
You're merely skin and bones. Are you obsessed
Like me, a victim of some god's grim jest?
So Euxitheus took you by surprise,
The rogue who gazed at beauty with both eyes!

LXXII   MELEAGER

Sweet dawn already! Sleepless on the porch
    Damis expires for Heraclitus, who
Has melted him like wax with eyes that scorch
    Like coals. Unlucky Damis, wake! I too
Have been hurt by carrying the torch
    For Love, and so I weep because you do.

LXXIII   CALLIMACHUS

Half of my soul still breathes, but I don't know
    If Love has rapt the other half away,
Or Death. Gone to some little gigolo?
    (I told the lads, "Rebuff the runaway.")
Look no further: that's where it would go,
    I'm sure, the ne'er-do-well, the *débauché*.

*Myiscus = "fly boy"

LXXIV   ΜΕΛΕΑΓΡΟΥ

Ἤν τι πάθω, Κλεόβουλε, (τὸ γὰρ πλέον ἐν πυρὶ παίδων
βαλλόμενος κεῖμαι λείψανον ἐν σποδιῇ·)
λίσσομαι, ἀκρήτῳ μέθυσον, πρὶν ὑπὸ χθόνα θέσθαι,
κάλπιν, ἐπιγράψας "Δῶρον Ἔρως Ἀΐδῃ."

LXXV   ΑΣΚΛΗΠΙΑΔΟΥ

Εἰ πτερά σοι προσέκειτο, καὶ ἐν χερὶ τόξα καὶ ἰοί,
οὐκ ἂν Ἔρως ἐγράφη Κύπριδος, ἀλλὰ σύ, παῖς.

LXXVI   ΜΕΛΕΑΓΡΟΥ

Εἰ μὴ τόξον Ἔρως, μηδὲ πτερά, μηδὲ φαρέτραν,
μηδὲ πυριβλήτους εἶχε πόθων ἀκίδας,
οὐκ, αὐτὸν τὸν πτανὸν ἐπόμνυμαι, οὔποτ᾽ ἂν ἔγνως
ἐκ μορφᾶς τίς ἔφυ Ζωΐλος ἢ τίς Ἔρως.

LXXVII   ΑΣΚΛΗΠΙΑΔΟΥ ἢ ΠΟΣΕΙΔΙΠΠΟΥ

Εἰ καθύπερθε λάβοις χρύσεα πτερά, καί σευ ἀπ᾽ ὤμων
τείνοιτ᾽ ἀργυρέων ἰοδόκος φαρέτρη,
καὶ σταίης παρ᾽ Ἔρωτα, φίλ᾽, ἀγλαόν, οὐ μὰ τὸν Ἑρμῆν,
οὐδ᾽ αὐτὴ Κύπρις γνώσεται ὃν τέτοκεν.

LXXVIII   ΜΕΛΕΑΓΡΟΥ

Εἰ χλαμύδ᾽ εἶχεν Ἔρως, καὶ μὴ πτερά, μηδ᾽ ἐπὶ νώτων
τόξα τε καὶ φαρέτραν, ἀλλ᾽ ἐφόρει πέτασον,
ναί, τὸν γαῦρον ἔφηβον ἐπόμνυμαι, Ἀντίοχος μὲν
ἦν ἂν Ἔρως, ὁ δ᾽ Ἔρως τἄμπαλιν Ἀντίοχος.

LXXIV   MELEAGER

If, Cleobulus, I should expire
Being cast on the juvenile pyre,
    As to ashes I burn
    Sprinkle wine on my urn
And inscribe it, " To Death from Desire."

LXXV   ASCLEPIADES

If you had wings, a bow, and arrows too,
I'd not think Cupid Venus' son, but you.

LXXVI   MELEAGER

If Cupid had no bow, no wings, and no
    Quiver filled with fiery arrows of
Desire, by looks alone you'd never know
    Zoilus from the wingèd god of love.

LXXVII   ASCLEPIADES *or* POSIDIPPUS

If you had golden wings, and from your shoulder
Dangled, dear, a silver arrow-holder,
And you stood next to Love in naked splendour,
Venus would wonder which did she engender.

LXXVIII   MELEAGER

If, instead of wings and a bow, Love had
    A mantle and a hat with a broad brim,
Antiochus—I swear by the proud lad
    Himself!—would look like Love, and Love like him.

LXXIX ΑΔΗΛΟΝ

Ἀντίπατρός μ᾽ ἐφίλησ᾽ ἤδη λήγοντος ἔρωτος,
καὶ πάλιν ἐκ ψυχρῆς πῦρ ἀνέκαυσε τέφρης·
δὶς δὲ μιῆς ἄκων ἔτυχον φλογός. ὦ δυσέρωτες,
φεύγετε, μὴ πρήσω τους πέλας ἁψάμενος.

LXXX ΜΕΛΕΑΓΡΟΥ

Ψυχὴ δυσδάκρυτε, τι σοι τὸ πεπανθὲν Ἔρωτος
τραῦμα διὰ σπλάγχνων αὖις ἀναφλέγεται;
μή, μή, πρὸς σὲ Διός, μή, πρὸς Διός, ὦ φιλάβουλε,
κινήσῃς τέφρῃ πῦρ ὑπολαμπόμενον.
αὐτίκα γάρ, λήθαργε κακῶν, πάλιν εἴ σε φυγοῦσαν
λήψετ᾽ Ἔρως, εὑρὼν δραπέτιν αἰκίσεται.

LXXXI ΜΕΛΕΑΓΡΟΥ

Ψυχαπάται δυσέρωτες, ὅσοι φλόγα τὰν φιλόπαιδα
οἴδατε, τοῦ πικροῦ γευσάμενοι μέλιτος,
ψυχρὸν ὕδωρ νιφάδα, ψυχρόν, τάχος, ἄρτι τακείης
ἐκ χιόνος τῇ ᾽μῇ χεῖτε περὶ κραδίῃ·
ἦ γὰρ ἰδεῖν ἔτλην Διονύσιον. ἀλλ᾽, ὁμόδουλοι,
πρὶν ψαῦσαι σπλάγχνων, πῦρ ἀπ᾽ ἐμεῦ σβέσατε.

LXXXII ΜΕΛΕΑΓΡΟΥ

Ἔσπευδον τὸν Ἔρωτα φυγεῖν· ὁ δὲ βαιὸν ἀνάψας
φανίον ἐκ τέφρης, εὑρέ με κρυπτόμενον·
κυκλώσας δ᾽ οὐ τόξα, χερὸς δ᾽ ἀκρώνυχα δισσόν,
κνίσμα πυρὸς θραύσας, εἰς μὲ λαθὼν ἔβαλεν·
ἐκ δὲ φλόγες πάντῃ μοι ἐπέδραμον. ὦ βραχυ φέγγος
λάμψαν ἐμοὶ μέγα πῦρ, Φανίον, ἐν κραδίᾳ.

LXXIX   ANONYMOUS

Antipater, when love began to pall,
      Kissed me, and from ashes stirred desire.
Twice burnt by the same flame, I warn off all
      Poor lovers, lest they touch me and catch fire.

LXXX   MELEAGER

Poor tearful spirit, does the dormant pain
Of love within your heart flare up again?
For God's sake, most irrational of souls,
Do not stir up those smouldering, banked coals!
Oblivious of your woes you got away,
But when Love catches you he'll make you pay.

LXXXI   MELEAGER

Unhappy, self-deceiving lovers who
Have known the bittersweet of boy-love too,
Pour round my heart cold water, quick, which flows,
My fellow slaves, from freshly melted snows.
At Dionysius I dared to gaze:
Before I am consumed put out the blaze.

LXXXII   MELEAGER

I tried to fly from Love, who snatched a brand
      Out of the coals and found my hiding place.
Bending, not his bow but his small hand,
      He flicked a pinch of fire in my face,
Enveloping me in flames. Sweet firebrand,
      Now you have made my heart your fireplace.

LXXXIII   ΜΕΛΕΑΓΡΟΥ

Οὔ μ' ἔτρωσεν Ἔρως τόξοις, οὐ λαμπάδ' ἀνάψας,
    ὡς πάρος, αἰθομέναν θῆκεν ὑπὸ κραδίᾳ·
σύγκωμον δὲ Πόθοισι φέρων Κύπριδος μυροφεγγὲς
    φανίον, ἄκρον ἐμοῖς ὄμμασι πῦρ ἔβαλεν·
ἐκ δέ με φέγγος ἔτηξε. τὸ δὲ βραχὺ φανίον ὤφθη
    πῦρ ψυχῆς τῇ 'μῇ καιόμενον κραδίᾳ.

LXXXIV   ΜΕΛΕΑΓΡΟΥ

Ὤνθρωποι, βωθεῖτε· τὸν ἐκ πελάγευς ἐπὶ γαῖαν
    ἄρτι με πρωτόπλουν ἴχνος ἐρειδόμενον
ἕλκει τῇδ' ὁ βίαιος Ἔρως· φλόγα δ' οἷα προφαίνων
    παιδὸς ἐπέστρεψεν κάλλος ἐραστὸν ἰδεῖν.
βαίνω δ' ἴχνος ἐπ' ἴχνος, ἐν ἀέρι δ' ἡδὺ τυπωθὲν
    εἶδος ἀφαρπάζων χείλεσιν ἡδὺ φιλῶ.
ἆρά γε τὴν πικρὰν προφυγὼν ἅλα, πουλύ τι κείνης
    πικρότερον χέρσῳ κῦμα περῶ Κύπριδος;

LXXXV   ΜΕΛΕΑΓΡΟΥ

Οἰνοπόται δέξασθε τὸν ἐκ πελάγευς, ἅμα πόντον
    καὶ κλῶπας προφυγόντ', ἐν χθονὶ δ' ὀλλύμενον.
ἄρτι γὰρ ἐκ νηός με μόνον πόδα θέντ' ἐπὶ γαῖαν
    ἀγρεύσας ἕλκει τῇδ' ὁ βίαιος Ἔρως,
ἐνθάδ' ὅπου τὸν παῖδα διαστείχοντ' ἐνόησα·
    αὐτομάτοις δ' ἄκων ποσσὶ ταχὺς φέρομαι.
κωμάζω δ' οὐκ οἶνον ὑπὸ φρένα, πῦρ δὲ γεμισθείς.
    ἀλλὰ φίλοι, ξεῖνοι, βαιὸν ἐπαρκέσατε,
ἀρκέσατ', ὦ ξεῖνοι, κἀμὲ Ξενίου πρὸς Ἔρωτος
    δέξασθ' ὀλλύμενον τὸν φιλίας ἱκέτην.

LXXXIII   MELEAGER

Love did not wound me with his normal dart;
He lit no blazing torch beneath my heart,
But in my eyes infused a fragrant fire,
Companion to disorderly Desire,
Melting me down: a tiny spark to start
This soulful conflagration in my heart!

LXXXIV   MELEAGER

Help! I have only to set foot on land,
Having survived my maiden voyage, and
Love drags me here by force and shines his light
On this boy's beauty: what a lovely sight!
I dog his steps, and grasping for his fair
Imaginary form, I kiss thin air.
Have I escaped the briny deep and found
Bitterer depths of longing on dry ground?

LXXXV   MELEAGER

Drunkards, make room for one who, safe ashore,
Escaped the sea, and pirates furthermore,
No sooner disembarked upon dry land
Than Love lays hold of me by brute force and
Drags me to see a certain boy pass by.
And here, averse, like a sleepwalker I
Stagger, not drunk with wine but with desire.
Give me a little help as I expire,
Dear strangers, take me in, a ruined guest,
For Love's sake honour friendship's last request.

40

LXXXVI   ΜΕΛΕΑΓΡΟΥ

Ἁ Κύπρις θήλεια γυναικομανὴ φλόγα βάλλει·
ἄρσενα δ᾽ αὐτὸς Ἔρως ἵμερον ἀνιοχεῖ.
ποῖ ῥέψω; ποτὶ παῖδ᾽ ἢ ματέρα; φαμὶ δὲ καὐτὰν
Κύπριν ἐρεῖν· "Νικᾷ τὸ θρασὺ παιδάριον."

LXXXVII   ΑΔΗΛΟΝ

Τλῆμον Ἔρως, οὐ θῆλυν ἐμοὶ πόθον, ἀλλά τιν᾽ αἰεὶ
δινεύεις στεροπὴν καύματος ἀρσενικοῦ.
ἄλλοτε γὰρ Δήμωνι πυρούμενος, ἄλλοτε λεύσσων
Ἰσμηνόν, δολιχοὺς αἰὲν ἔχω καμάτους.
οὐ μούνοις δ᾽ ἐπὶ τοῖσι δεδόρκαμεν· ἀλλ᾽ ἐπιπάντων
ἄρκυσι πουλυμανῆ κανθὸν ἐφελκόμεθα.

LXXXVIII   ΑΔΗΛΟΝ

Δισσοί με τρύχουσι καταιγίζοντες ἔρωτες,
Εὔμαχε, καὶ δισσαῖς ἐνδέδεμαι μανίαις·
ἧ μὲν ἐπ᾽ Ἀσάνδρου κλίνω δέμας, ἧ δὲ πάλιν μοι
ὀφθαλμὸς νεύει Τηλέφου ὀξύτερος.
τμήξατ᾽, ἐμοὶ τοῦφ᾽ ἡδύ, καὶ εἰς πλάστιγγα δικαίην
νειμάμενοι, κλήρῳ τἀμὰ φέρεσθε μέλη.

LXXXIX   ΑΔΗΛΟΝ

Κύπρι, τί μοι τρισσοὺς ἐφ᾽ ἕνα σκοπὸν ἤλασας ἰούς,
ἐν δὲ μιῇ ψυχῇ τρισσὰ πέπηγε βέλη;
καὶ τῇ μὲν φλέγομαι, τῇ δ᾽ ἕλκομαι· ἧ δ᾽ ἀπονεύσω,
διστάζω, λάβρῳ δ᾽ ἐν πυρὶ πᾶς φλέγομαι.

LXXXVI   MELEAGER

Lady Venus generates our lust
    For females; Cupid pricks desire for males.
Which shall I turn to? Even Venus must
    Admit her cheeky little brat prevails.

LXXXVII   ANONYMOUS

Brash Love, you make me dizzy! Do I yearn
For women? No, for my own sex I burn.
Enflamed by Damon, every time I see
Ismenus I am plunged in misery.
I stare at others too; my roving eye
Is caught by every boy who passes by.

LXXXVIII   ANONYMOUS

Two tempestuous passions having ground
Me down, in double madness I am bound.
As soon as to Asander's person I
Incline, Telephus' catches my keen eye.
How nice it would be if they could divide
Me equally, and then let chance decide!

LXXXIX   ANONYMOUS

Why, Venus, must you take a triple shot
    At me, and lodge three arrows in my soul?
I'm pulled this way and that, and don't know what
    I want; this rabid fire consumes me whole.

42

XC ΑΔΗΛΟΝ

Οὐκέτ᾽ ἐρῶ. πεπάλαικα πόθοις τρισίν· εἷς μὲν ἑταίρης,
εἷς δέ με παρθενικῆς, εἷς δέ μ᾽ ἔκαυσε νέου·
καὶ κατὰ πᾶν ἤλγηκα. γεγύμνασμαι μέν, ἑταίρης
πείθων τὰς ἐχθρὰς οὐδὲν ἔχοντι θύρας·
ἔστρωμαι δὲ κόρης ἐπὶ παστάδος αἰὲν ἄϋπνος,
ἓν τὸ ποθεινότατον παιδὶ φίλημα διδούς.
οἴμοι· πῶς εἴπω πῦρ τὸ τρίτον; ἐκ γὰρ ἐκείνου
βλέμματα καὶ κενεὰς ἐλπίδας οἶδα μόνον.

XCI ΠΟΛΥΣΤΡΑΤΟΥ

Δισσὸς Ἔρως αἴθει ψυχὴν μίαν. ὦ τὰ περισσὰ
ὀφθαλμοὶ πάντη πάντα κατοσσόμενοι,
εἴδετε τὸν χρυσέαισι περίσκεπτον χαρίτεσσιν
Ἀντίοχον, λιπαρῶν ἄνθεμον ἠϊθέων.
ἀρκείτω· τί τὸν ἡδὺν ἐπηυγάσσασθε καὶ ἁβρὸν
Στασικράτη, Παφίης ἔρνος ἰοστεφάνου;
καίεσθε, τρύχεσθε, καταφλέχθητέ ποτ᾽ ἤδη·
οἱ δύο γὰρ ψυχὴν οὐκ ἂν ἔλοιτε μίαν.

XCII ΜΕΛΕΑΓΡΟΥ

Ὦ προδόται ψυχῆς, παίδων κύνες, αἰὲν ἐν ἰξῷ
Κύπριδος ὀφθαλμοὶ βλέμματα χριόμενοι,
ἡρπάσατ᾽ ἄλλον Ἔρωτ᾽, ἄρνες λύκον, οἷα κορώνη
σκορπίον, ὡς τέφρη πῦρ ὑποθαλπόμενον.
δρᾶθ᾽ ὅ τι καὶ βούλεσθε. τί μοι νενοτισμένα χεῖτε
δάκρυα, πρὸς δ᾽ Ἱκέτην αὐτομολεῖτε τάχος;
ὀπτᾶσθ᾽ ἐν κάλλει, τύφεσθ᾽ ὑποκαόμενοι νῦν,
ἄκρος ἐπεὶ ψυχῆς ἐστι μάγειρος Ἔρως.

XC   ANONYMOUS

I'm through with love! Three bad upsets I've had:
A courtesan, a maiden, and a lad,
All painful. Long did I besiege the whore's
Door, which was posted, NO SOLICITORS,
And lying sleepless in a colonnade,
I showered longing kisses on the maid;
Ah, how describe the third? From him, as yet,
Glances and promises are all I get.

XCI   POLYSTRATUS

Two loves consume my soul. I, having gone
Everywhere looking for a paragon,
Spotted Antiochus, whose charm enjoys
Preeminence among our golden boys.
That should suffice! Why seek a younger one,
Delicious Stasicrates, Venus' son?
The pair of you are helpless to control
What you may well destroy, this single soul.

XCII   MELEAGER

My eyes give me away, those boy-hounds who
Stick ever to their quarry's tracks like glue!
As sheep catch wolves, and fuel catches fire,
As birds catch snakes, you've caught your new desire.
Do as you please. But why shed tears like rain,
Then run right after Hiketas again?
Go on and baste yourself in his good looks:
Love is the chef of sentimental cooks.

XCIII   ΡΙΑΝΟΥ

Οἱ παῖδες λαβύρινθος ἀνέξοδος· ᾗ γὰρ ἂν ὄμμα
ῥίψῃς, ὡς ἰξῷ τοῦτο προσαμπέχεται.
τῇ μὲν γὰρ Θεόδωρος ἄγει ποτὶ πίονα σαρκὸς
ἀκμὴν καὶ γυίων ἄνθος ἀκηράσιον·
τῇ δὲ Φιλοκλῆος χρύσεον ῥέθος, ὃς τὸ καθ᾽ ὕχος
οὐ μέγας, οὐρανίη δ᾽ ἀμφιτέθηλε χάρις.
ἢν δ᾽ ἐπὶ Λεπτίνεω στρέψῃς δέμας, οὐκέτι γυῖα
κινήσεις, ἀλύτῳ δ᾽ ὡς ἀδάμαντι μενεῖς
ἴχνια κολληθείς· τοῖον σέλας ὄμμασιν αἴθει
κοῦρος καὶ νεάτους ἐκ κορυφῆς ὄνυχας.
χαίρετε καλοὶ παῖδες, ἐς ἀκμαίην δὲ μόλοιτε
ἥβην, καὶ λευκὴν ἀμφιέσαισθε κόμην.

XCIV   ΜΕΛΕΑΓΡΟΥ

Τερπνὸς μὲν Διόδωρος, ἐν ὄμμασι δ᾽ Ἡράκλειτος,
ἡδυεπὴς δὲ Δίων, ὀσφύϊ δ᾽ Οὐλιάδης.
ἀλλὰ σὺ μὲν ψαύοις ἀπαλόχροος, ᾧ δέ, Φιλόκλεις,
ἔμβλεπε, τῷ δὲ λάλει, τὸν δὲ ... τὸ λειπόμενον·
ὡς γνῷς οἷος ἐμὸς νόος ἄφθονος· ἢν δὲ Μυΐσκῳ
λίχνος ἐπιβλέχῃς, μηκέτ᾽ ἴδοις τὸ καλόν.

XCIII   RHIANUS

Boys are an inextricable maze;
Like glue they hold the transitory gaze.
Here Theodorus' carnal charms attract
You, limbs so round and firm and fully packed;
Here golden-skinned Philocles, who is all
Heavenly grace, although not very tall.
If on Leptinus' form your eyes you cast,
You cannot budge, your feet will be stuck fast
As adamant; that youngster's looks are so
Ardent they'll kindle you from top to toe.
Hail, lovely boys! May you attain your prime,
And live until your hair turns white with time.

XCIV   MELEAGER

Diodorus is a living treasure,
      Heraclitus always seems on view,
Dion's conversation gives much pleasure,
      So does Uliades' backside, too!
Stroke the delicate-complexioned boy,
      Ogle him you find the prettiest;
Chat up the chatterbox, and then enjoy
      The favours of the favoured . . . and all the rest.
You know I do not have a jealous nature,
      Philocles, but if you presume to cast
Lecherous glances on Myiscus' ass, your
      Glimpse of beauty might well be your last.

XCV ΜΕΛΕΑΓΡΟΥ

Εἴ σε Πόθοι στέργουσι, Φιλόκλεες, ἤ τε μυρόπνους
Πειθώ, καὶ κάλλευς ἀνθολόγοι Χάριτες,
ἀγκὰς ἔχοις Διόδωρον, ὁ δὲ γλυκὺς ἀντίος ἄδοι
Δωρόθεος, κείσθω δ᾽ εἰς γόνυ Καλλικράτης,
ἰαίνοι δὲ Δίων τόδ᾽ ἐΰστοχον ἐν χερὶ τείνων
σὸν κέρας, Οὐλιάδης δ᾽ αὐτὸ περισκυθίσαι,
δοίη δ᾽ ἡδὺ φίλημα Φίλων, Θήρων δὲ λαλῆσαι,
θλίβοις δ᾽ Εὐδήμου τιτθὸν ὑπὸ χλαμύδι.
εἰ γάρ σοι τάδε τερπνὰ πόροι θεός, ὦ μάκαρ, οἵαν
ἀρτύσεις παίδων Ῥωμαϊκὴν λοπάδα.

XCVI ΑΔΗΛΟΝ

Οὔτι μάταν θνατοῖσι φάτις τοιάδε βοᾶται,
ὡς "οὐ πάντα θεοὶ πᾶσιν ἔδωκαν ἔχειν."
εἶδος μὲν γάρ ἄμωμον, ἐπ᾽ ὄμμασι δ᾽ ἁ περίσαμος
αἰδώς, καὶ στέρνοις ἀμφιτέθαλε χάρις,
οἷσι καὶ ἠϊθέσυς ἐπιδάμνασαι· ἀλλ᾽ ἐπὶ ποσσὶν
οὐκέτι τὰν αὐτὰν δῶκαν ἔχειν σε χάριν.
πλὴν κρηπὶς κρύψει ποδὸς ἴχνιον, ὠγαθὲ Πύρρε,
κάλλεϊ δὲ σφετέρῳ τέρψει ἀγαλλόμενον.

XCVII ΑΝΤΙΠΑΤΡΟΥ

Εὐπάλαμος ξανθὸν μὲν ἐρεύθεται, ἶσον Ἔρωτι,
μέσφα ποτὶ Κρητῶν ποιμένα Μηριόνην·
ἐκ δέ νυ Μηριόνεω Ποδαλείριος οὐκέτ᾽ ἐς Ἠὼ
νεῖται· ἴδ᾽ ὡς φθονερὰ παγγενέτειρα φύσις.
εἰ γὰρ τῷ τά τ᾽ ἔνερθε τά θ᾽ ὑψόθεν ἶσα πέλοιτο,
ἦν ἂν Ἀχιλλῆος φέρτερος Αἰακίδεω.

XCV   MELEAGER

Philocles, if Desire, sweet Blandishment,
And the Graces, beauty's botanists, consent,
Embracing Diodorus may you see
Sweet Dorotheus singing vis-à-vis,
While holding Callicrates on your knee;
May Dion's little fingers hotly grip
Your horny prick, which Uliades' strip;
May you share Philo's kiss and Thero's talk,
And feel Eudemus up beneath his smock.
If, blessèd man, god granted you such joys,
You'd have arranged a smorgasbord of boys.

XCVI   ANONYMOUS

There's truth in the old adage, that the gods
Do not give everybody the same odds.
Your form is flawless, modesty shines in
Your eyes, a charming bloom is on your skin,
Surpassing other youths. But for your feet,
All this god-given grace would be complete.
But, Pyrrhus, slip your foot into this shoe—
It will embellish and astonish you.

XCVII   ANTIPATER

Eupalamas—or Lilyfoot—above
His waistline blushes roseate as Love;
However, dawn does not extend from his
Waist down. How stingy Mother Nature is!
Were his bottom and his top the same,
He'd put Achilles' bronze physique to shame.

48

XCVIII ΠΟΣΕΙΔΙΠΠΟΥ

Τὸν Μουσῶν τέττιγα Πόθος δήσας ἐπ᾿ ἀκάνθαις
κοιμίζειν ἐθέλει, πῦρ ὑπὸ πλευρὰ βαλών·
ἡ δὲ πρὶν ἐν βίβλοις πεπονημένη ἀλλ᾿ ἀθερίζει
ψυχή, ἀνιηρῷ δαίμονι μεμφομένη.

XCIX ΑΔΗΛΟΝ

Ἠγρεύθην ὑπ᾿ Ἔρωτος ὁ μηδ᾿ ὄναρ, οὐδ᾿ ἔμαθον
περ ἄρσενα ποιμαίνειν θερμὸν ὑπὸ κραδίας,
ἠγρεύθην. ἀλλ᾿ οὔ με κακῶν πόθος, ἀλλ᾿ ἀκέραιον
σύντροφον αἰσχύνῃ βλέμμα κατηνθράκισεν.
τηκέσθω Μουσέων ὁ πολὺς πόνος· ἐν πυρὶ γὰρ νοῦς
βέβληται, γλυκερῆς ἄχθος ἔχων ὀδύνης.

C ΑΔΗΛΟΝ

Εἰς οἵων με πόθων λιμένα ξένον, ὦ Κύπρι, θεῖσα
οὐκ ἐλεεῖς, καὐτὴ πεῖραν ἔχουσα πόνων;
ἦ μ᾿ ἐθέλεις ἄτλητα παθεῖν καὶ τοῦτ᾿ ἔπος εἰπεῖν,
"Τὸν σοφὸν ἐν Μούσαις Κύπρις ἔτρωσε μόνη";

CI ΜΕΛΕΑΓΡΟΥ

Τόν με Πόθοις ἄτρωτον ὑπὸ στέρνοισι Μυΐσκος
ὄμμασι τοξεύσας, τοῦτ᾿ ἐβόησεν ἔπος·
"Τὸν θρασὺν εἷλον ἐγώ· τὸ δ᾿ ἐπ᾿ ὀφρύσι κεῖνο φρύαγμα
σκηπτροφόρου σοφίας ἠνίδε ποσσὶ πατῶ."
τῷ δ᾿, ὅσον ἀμπνεύσας, τόδ᾿ ἔφην· "Φίλε κοῦρε, τί θαμβεῖς;
καὐτὸν ἀπ᾿ Οὐλύμπου Ζῆνα καθεῖλεν Ἔρως."

CII ΚΑΛΛΙΜΑΧΟΥ

Ὠγρευτής, Ἐπίκυδες, ἐν οὔρεσι πάντα λαγωὸν
διφᾷ, καὶ πάσης ἴχνια δορκαλίδος,

XCVIII   POSIDIPPUS

Binding the poet's soul with briars, Desire
Tries to relax it over a slow fire,
But the hard-working bookworm still makes light
Of everything but this malicious sprite.

XCIX   ANONYMOUS

I'm caught by Love. I never dreamt I'd learn
With ardour for another male to burn.
I'm caught, yet sinful passion played no part:
A pure and modest glance enflamed my heart.
My labour for the Muses—all in vain!
My mind, on fire, is fraught with dulcet pain.

C   ANONYMOUS

To what strange port of longings, pitiless
     Venus, towards love's pain, well though you know it,
You've brought me, in unbearable distress
     To protest, "None but Venus hurt this poet"!

CI   MELEAGER

Transfixing with a look my unscathed heart,
Myiscus cried, "I've caught the brash upstart!
Behold how underfoot I trample now
The pride of regal wisdom on his brow!"
I gasped, "Dear boy, why should you feel surprise?
Love dragged great Zeus himself down from the skies."

CII   CALLIMACHUS

After each mountain hare the hunstman goes,
Tracking each doe's footprints through frosts and snows,

στίβνι καὶ νιφετῷ κεχρημένος. ἢν δέ τις εἴπνι,
"Τῆ, τόδε βέβληται θηρίον," οὐκ ἔλαβεν.
χοὐμὸς ἔρως τοιόσδε· τὰ μὲν φεύγοντα διώκειν
οιτε, τὰ δ᾽ ἐν μέσσῳ κείμενα παρπέταται.

CIII   ΑΔΗΛΟΝ

Οἶδα φιλεῖν φιλέοντας· ἐπίσταμαι, ἤν μ᾽ ἀδικῇ τις,
μισεῖν· ἀμφοτέρων εἰμὶ γὰρ οὐκ ἀδαής.

CIV   ΑΔΗΛΟΝ

Οὑμὸς ἔρως παρ᾽ ἐμοὶ μενέτω μόνον· ἢν δὲ πρὸς ἄλλους
φοιτήσῃ, μισῶ κοινὸν ἔρωτα, Κύπρι.

CV   ΑΣΚΛΗΠΙΑΔΟΥ

Μικρὸς Ἔρως ἐκ μητρὸς ἔτ᾽ εὐθήρατος ἀποπτάς,
ἐξ οἴκων ὑψοῦ Δάμιδος οὐ πέτομαι·
ἀλλ᾽ αὐτοῦ, φιλέων τε καὶ ἀζήλωτα φιληθείς,
οὐ πολλοῖς, εὐκρὰς δ᾽ εἰς ἑνὶ συμφέρομαι.

CVI   ΜΕΛΕΑΓΡΟΥ

Ἓν καλὸν οἶδα τὸ πᾶν, ἕν μοι μόνον οἶδε τὸ λίχνον
ὄμμα, Μυΐσκον ὁρᾶν· τἄλλα δὲ τυφλὸς ἐγώ.
πάντα δ᾽ ἐκεῖνος ἐμοὶ φαντάζεται· ἆρ᾽ ἐσορῶσιν
ὀφθαλμοὶ ψυχῇ προς χάριν, οἱ κόλακες;

CVII   ΑΔΗΛΟΝ

Τὸν καλόν, ὦ Χάριτες, Διονύσιον, εἰ μὲν ἔλοιτο
τἀμά, καὶ εἰς ὥρας αὖθις ἄγοιτε καλόν·
εἰ δ᾽ ἕτερον στέρξειε παρεὶς ἐμέ, μύρτον ἔωλον
ἐρρίφθω ξηροῖς φυρόμενον σκυβάλοις.

But any stricken creature he descries
He does not bag. My love, perverse likewise,
Understands how to chase the fleet and shy
Game, but what's obvious it passes by.

CIII   ANONYMOUS

I give back love for love and hate for hate,
Completely ignorant of neither state.

CIV   ANONYMOUS

I want my love exclusive. If it strays,
Venus, I hate a love with common ways.

CV   ASCLEPIADES

A little Love, I left my mother's home;
Easily caught, from Damis' I don't roam,
Loving, beloved, (rivals I have none),
Commingling not with many but with one.

CVI   MELEAGER

Myiscus' looks are all my avid eyes
Know how to dote on, sightless otherwise.
He's all my fantasy. Must every glance
Flatter the soul? Must eyes be psychophants?

CVII   ANONYMOUS

If comely Dionysius picks me,
    May The Graces keep him ever fair!
But should he pass me over heartlessly,
    Good riddance to bad rubbish, I declare.

CVIII   ΔΙΟΝΥΣΙΟΥ

Εἰ μὲν ἐμὲ στέρξεις, εἴης ἰσόμοιρος, Ἄκρατε,
   Χίῳ, καὶ Χίου πουλὺ μελιχρότερος·
εἰ δ᾽ ἕτερον κρίναις ἐμέθεν πλέον, ἀμφὶ σὲ βαίη
   κώνωψ ὀξηρῷ τυφόμενος κεράμῳ.

CIX   ΜΕΛΕΑΓΡΟΥ

Ὁ τρυφερὸς Διόδωρος ἐς ἠϊθέους φλόγα βάλλων
   ἤγρευται λαμυροῖς ὄμμασι Τιμαρίου,
τὸ γλυκύπικρον Ἔρωτος ἔχων βέλος. ἦ τόδε καινὸν
   θάμβος ὁρῶ· φλέγεται πῦρ πυρὶ καιόμενον.

CX   ΜΕΛΕΑΓΡΟΥ

Ἤστραψε γλυκὺ κάλλος· ἰδοὺ φλόγας ὄμμασι βάλλει.
   ἆρα κεραυνομάχαν ταῖδ᾽ ἀνέδειξεν Ἔρως;
χαῖρε Πόθων ἀκτῖνα φέρων θνατοῖσι, Μυΐσκε,
   καὶ λάμποις ἐπὶ γᾷ πυρσὸς ἐμοὶ φίλιος.

CXI   ΑΔΗΛΟΝ

Πτανὸς Ἔρως, σὺ δὲ ποσσὶ ταχύς· τὸ δὲ κάλλος ὁμοῖον
   ἀμφοτέρων. τόξοις, Εὔβιε, λειπόμεθα.

CXII   ΑΔΗΛΟΝ

Εὐφαμεῖτε νέοι· τὸν Ἔρωτ᾽ ἄγει Ἀρκεσίλαος,
   πορφυρέῃ δήσας Κύπριδος ἀρπεδόνῃ.

CXIII   ΜΕΛΕΑΓΡΟΥ

Καὐτὸς Ἔρως ὁ πτανὸς ἐν αἰθέρι δέσμιος ἥλω,
   ἀγρευθεὶς τοῖς σοῖς ὄμμασι, Τιμάριον.

CVIII   DIONYSIUS

Acrastus, if you care for me, you are
    Like unmixed Chian wine, but sweeter still.
    If you choose someone else, I hope you will
Turn musty as a jar of vinegar.

CIX   MELEAGER

Is tender Diodorus, who turned on
    Our youth, transfixed by bittersweet desire,
Enflamed by lickerish Timarion?
    A novel marvel: fighting fire with fire.

CX   MELEAGER

His eyes flash beauty sweet enough to scorch:
    Does Love equip young boys with thunderbolts?
    Bringing a sexy gleam to mortal dolts,
Myiscus, shine on earth, my darling torch.

CXI   ANONYMOUS

While Love has wings, you're swift of foot. You're cute
As well. A pity that you cannot shoot!

CXII   ANONYMOUS

Be quiet, lads! Archesilaus to bring
Love here, bound him with Venus' crimson string.

CXIII   MELEAGER

Timarion you snared, by fluttering
Your eyelids, Love, and caught him on the wing.

CXIV ΜΕΛΕΑΓΡΟΥ

Ἠοῦς ἄγγελε, χαῖρε, Φαεσφόρε, καὶ ταχὺς ἔλθοις
Ἕσπερος, ἣν ἀπάγεις, λάθριος αὖθις ἄγων.

CXV ΑΔΗΛΟΝ

Ἄκρητον μανίην ἔπιον· μεθύων μέγα μύθοις
ὥπλισμαι πολλὴν εἰς ὁδὸν ἀφροσύναν.
κωμάσομαι· τί δέ μοι βροντέων μέλει, ἢ τί κεραυνῶν;
ἢν βάλλῃ, τὸν ἔρωθ' ὅπλον ἄτρωτον ἔχων.

CXVI ΑΔΗΛΟΝ

Κωμάσομαι· μεθύω γὰρ ὅλος μέγα. παῖ, λάβε τοῦτον
τὸν στέφανον, τὸν ἐμοῖς δάκρυσι λουόμενον·
μακρὴν δ' οὐχὶ μάτην ὁδὸν ἵξομαι· ἔστι δ' ἀωρὶ
καὶ σκότος· ἀλλὰ μέγας φανὸς ἐμοὶ Θεμίσων.

CXVII ΜΕΛΕΑΓΡΟΥ

Βεβλήσθω κύβος· ἅπτε· πορεύσομαι. Ἠνίδε, τόλμα,
οἰνοβαρές. Τίν' ἔχεις φροντίδα; κωμάσομαι.
κωμάσομαι; Ποῖ, θυμέ, τρέπῃ; Τί δ' ἔρωτι λογισμός;
ἅπτε τάχος. Ποῦ δ' ἡ πρόσθε λόγων μελέτη;
Ἐρρίφθω σοφίας ὁ πολὺς πόνος· ἓν μόνον οἶδα
τοῦθ', ὅτι καὶ Ζηνὸς λῆμα καθεῖλεν Ἔρως.

CXVIII ΚΑΛΛΙΜΑΧΟΥ

Εἰ μὲν ἑκών, Ἀρχῖν', ἐπεκώμασα, μυρία μεμφου·
εἰ δ' ἀέκων ἥκω, τὴν προπέτειαν ὅρα·
ἄκρητος καὶ ἔρως μ' ἠνάγκασαν· ὧν ὁ μὲν αὐτῶν
εἷλκεν, ὁ δ' οὐκ εἴα σώφρονα θυμὸν ἔχειν.
ἐλθὼν δ' οὐκ ἐβόησα, τίς ἢ τίνος, ἀλλ' ἐφίλησα
τὴν φλιήν· εἰ τοῦτ' ἔστ' ἀδίκημ', ἀδικῶ.

CXIV   MELEAGER

Hail, morning star, fair messenger of dawn!
As evening star, bring back the sweet cheat gone.

CXV   ANONYMOUS

Having imbibed pure madness, I am made
    Tipsy by words, by drunken folly armed.
So what if it thunders on my serenade?
    Love's body armour will keep me unharmed.

CXVI   ANONYMOUS

I'll serenade him absolutely stewed:
"Accept, dear boy, this wreath with tears bedewed."
Go all that way for nothing? Though the night
Is dark, Themison is my guiding light.

CXVII   MELEAGER

That's settled. Light the lights, I'm on my way.—
Drink makes you bold.—Why worry? I'll go pay
Him court.—*Your wit's astray.*—Does love allow
Reason? Lights, quick!—*Where is your logic now?*
Forget the quest for wisdom! All I know,
Is, Love brought Zeus' lofty spirit low.

CXVIII   CALLIMACHUS

Scold me, Archinus, for my headstrong wooing,
Or call your magnetism my undoing.
Strong drink moved me, and love, which drew my soul,
While drinking robbed me of all self-control.
I kissed your door but did not shout my name
Or yours. If that's a crime, I am to blame.

CXIX   ΜΕΛΕΑΓΡΟΥ

Οἴσω, ναὶ μὰ σέ, Βάκχε, τὸ σὸν θράσος· ἁγέο, κώμων
ἄρχε· θεὸς θνατὰν ἀνιοχεῖ κραδίαν·
ἐν πυρὶ γενναθεὶς στέργεις φλόγα τὰν ἐν ἔρωτι,
καὶ με πάλιν δήσας τὸν σὸν ἄγεις ἱκέτην.
ἦ προδότας κἄπιστος ἔφυς· τεὰ δ' ὄργια κρύπτειν
αὐδῶν, ἐκφαίνειν τἀμὰ σὺ νῦν ἐθέλεις.

CXX   ΠΟΣΕΙΔΙΠΠΟΥ

Εὐπλῶ, καὶ πρὸς σὲ μαχήσομαι, οὐδ' ἀπεροῦμαι
θνητὸς ἐών· σὺ δ', Ἔρως, μηκέτι μοι πρόσαγε.
ἤν με λάβῃς μεθύοντ', ἄπαγ' ἔκδοτον· ἄχρι δὲ νήφω,
τὸν παραταξάμενον πρὸς σὲ λογισμὸν ἔχω.

CXXI   ΡΙΑΝΟΥ

Ἦ ῥά νύ τοι, Κλεόνικε, δι' ἀτραπιτοῖο κιόντι
στεινῆς ἤντησαν ταὶ λιπαραὶ Χάριτες·
καί σε ποτὶ ῥοδέαισιν ἐπηχύναντο χέρεσσιν,
κοῦρε; πεποίησαι δ' ἡλίκος ἐσσὶ χάρις.
τηλόθι μοι μάλα χαῖρε· πυρὸς δ' οὐκ ἀσφαγὲς ἄσσον
ἕρπειν αὐηρήν, ἃ φίλος, ἀνθέρικα.

CXXII   ΜΕΛΕΑΓΡΟΥ

Ὦ Χάριτες, τὸν καλὸν Ἀρισταγόρην ἐσιδοῦσαι
ἀντίον, εἰς τρυφερὰς ἠγκαλίσασθε χέρας·
οὕνεκα καὶ μορφᾷ βάλλει φλόγα, καὶ γλυκυμυθεῖ
καίρια, καὶ σιγῶν ὄμμασι τερπνὰ λαλεῖ.
τηλόθι μοι πλάζοιτο. τί δὲ πλέον; ὡς γὰρ Ὄλυμπον
Ζεὺς νέον οἶδεν ὁ παῖς μακρὰ κεραυνοβολεῖν.

CXIX   MELEAGER

I'll tolerate your rudeness, Bacchus. Start
The party, god that rules the human heart.
Born from the fire, you love love's flame; enchain
Me as your faithful follower again.
Perfidiously you tell me to conceal
Your mysteries, yet mine you would reveal.

CXX   POSIDIPPUS

I'll take up arms and never will say die,
    Mere mortal though I am. Love, stay your hand!
While you may capture me when drunk, when I
    Am sober, I have reason at command.

CXXI   RHIANUS

Traipsing some narow pathway did the Graces,
Cleonicus, meet you with shining faces,
And take you in their rosy-armed embrace
Making of you an honorary Grace?
I'll keep my distance, thank you: tinder near
A fire would be in jeopardy, my dear.

CXXII   MELEAGER

Staring Aristagoras in the face,
The Graces clasped him in a fond embrace,
His beauty blazes now, his talk is sweet,
When mute his smiling eyes are indiscreet.
I wish he'd go away! But what's the use?
He throws his thunderbolts as far as Zeus.

CXXIII ΑΔΗΛΟΝ

Πυγμῇ νικησαντα τὸν Ἀντικλέους Μενέχαρμον
λημνίσκοις μαλακοῖς ἐστεφάνωσα δέκα,
καὶ τρισσῶς ἐφίλησα πεφυρμένον αἵματι πολλῷ·
ἀλλ᾽ ἐμοὶ ἦν σμύρνης κεῖνο μελιχρότερον.

CXXIV ΑΔΗΛΟΝ, οἱ δὲ ΑΡΤΕΜΩΝΟΣ

Λάθρη παπταίνοντα παρὰ φλιὴν Ἐχέδημον
λάθριος ἀκρήβην τὸν χαρίεντ᾽ ἔκυσα.
δειμαίνων καὶ γάρ μοι ἐνύπνιος ἦλθε φαρέτρην
αἰταίων καὶ δοὺς ᾤχετ᾽ ἀλεκτρυόνας,
ἄλλοτε μειδιόων, ὁτὲ δ᾽ οὐ φίλος. ἀλλὰ μελισσέων
ἐσμοῦ καὶ κνίδης καὶ πυρὸς ἠψάμεθα;

CXXV ΜΕΛΕΑΓΡΟΥ

Ἡδύ τί μοι διὰ νυκτὸς ἐνύπνιον ἁβρὰ γελῶντος
ὀκτωκαιδεκέτους παιδὸς ἔτ᾽ ἐν χλαμύδι
ἤγαγ᾽ Ἔρως ὑπὸ χλαῖναν· ἐγὼ δ᾽ ἁπαλῷ περὶ χρωτὶ
στέρνα βαλὼν κενεὰς ἐλπίδας ἐδρεπόμαν.
καί μ᾽ ἔτι νῦν θάλπει μνήμης πόθος· ὄμμασι δ᾽ ὕπνον
ἀγρευτὴν πτηνοῦ φάσματος αἰὲν ἔχω.
ὦ δύσερως ψυχή, παῦσαί ποτε καὶ δι᾽ ὀνείρων
εἰδώλοις κάλλευς κωφὰ χλιαινομένη.

CXXVI ΜΕΛΕΑΓΡΟΥ

Ἦρκταί μευ κραδίας ψαύειν πόνος· ἦ γὰρ ἀλύων
ἀκρονυχεὶ ταύταν ἔκνισ᾽ ὁ θερμὸς Ἔρως·
εἶπε δὲ μειδήσας· ᾽᾽Ἕξεις πάλι τὸ γλυκὺ τραῦμα,
ὦ δύσερως, λάβρῳ καιόμενος μέλιτι.᾽᾽
ἐξ οὗ δὴ νέον ἔρνος ἐν ἠϊθέοις Διόφαντον
λεύσσων οὔτε φυγεῖν οὔτε μένειν δύναμαι.

CXXIII   ANONYMOUS

I crowned young Menecharmus, when he gained
    The title, with the wreath of victory,
And kissed him, too, though he was all blood-stained:
    That blood seemed sweeter than perfume to me!

CXXIV   ARTEMON?

Seeing young Echedemus sneak a peek
Outdoors, I slyly kissed the little sneak.
Then, dressed like Cupid, in a dream he shocks
Me with the present of two fighting cocks.
Now smiling, now unfriendly. Did I seize
Fire or a thistle or a swarm of bees?

CXXV   MELEAGER

Love brought between my sheets a laughing lad
One night. Eighteen years old, he was half-clad,
Like a young boy: what a sweet dream! I pressed
Smooth flesh in desperation to my breast.
Warmed by that lustful memory, I keep
Before my eyes phantasmagoric sleep.
When will my lovesick soul in dreams refrain
From chafing beauty's images in vain?

CXXVI   MELEAGER

Now I have just begun to feel the pain:
Hot, errant Love has scratched my heart again.
Smirking he said, "Poor lover, you will bear
The sentimental brand of sweet despair."
Nor can I, when amongst the boyish band
I spot young Diophantes, stir or stand.

60

CXXVII   ΜΕΛΕΑΓΡΟΥ

Εἰνόδιον στείχοντα μεσαμβρινὸν εἶδον Ἄλεξιν,
   ἄρτι κόμαν καρπῶν κειρομένου θέρεος.
διπλαῖ δ᾽ ἀκτῖνές με κατέφλεγον· αἱ μὲν Ἔρωτος,
   παιδὸς ἀπ᾽ ὀφθαλμῶν, αἱ δὲ παρ᾽ ἠελίου.
ἀλλ᾽ ἃς μὲν νὺξ αὖθις ἐκοίμισεν· ἃς δ᾽ ἐν ὀνείροις
   εἴδωλον μορφῆς μᾶλλον ἀνεφλόγισεν.
λυσίπονος δ᾽ ἑτέροις ἐπ᾽ ἐμοὶ πόνον ὕπνος ἔτευξεν
   ἔμπνουν πῦρ ψυχῇ κάλλος ἀπεικονίσας.

CXXVIII   ΜΕΛΕΑΓΡΟΥ

Αἰπολικαὶ σύριγγες, ἐν οὔρεσι μηκέτι Δάφνιν
   φωνεῖτ᾽, αἰγιβάτῃ Πανὶ χαριζόμεναι·
μηδὲ σὺ τὸν στεφθέντα, λύρη, Φοίβοιο προφῆτι,
   δάφνῃ παρθενίῃ μέλφ᾽ Ὑάκινθον ἔτι.
ἦν γὰρ ὅτ᾽ ἦν Δάφνις μὲν ἐν οὔρεσι σοὶδ᾽ Ὑάκινθος
   τερπνός· νῦν δὲ Πόθων σκῆπτρα Δίων ἐχέτω.

CXXIX   ΑΡΑΤΟΥ

Ἀργεῖος Φιλοκλῆς Ἄργει "καλός·" αἳ δὲ Κορίνθου
   στῆλαι, καὶ Μεγαρέων ταὐτὸ βοῶσι τάθοι·
γέγραπται καὶ μέχρι λοετρῶν Ἀμφιαράου,
   ὡς καλός. ἀλλ᾽ ὀλίγον· γράμμασι λειπόμεθα·
τῷδ᾽ οὐ γὰρ πέτραι ἐπιμάρτυρες, ἀλλὰ Ῥηνὸς
   αὐτὸς ἰδών· ἑτέρου δ᾽ ἐστὶ περισσότερος.

CXXX   ΑΔΗΛΟΝ

Εἶπα, καὶ αὖ πάλιν εἶπα· "Καλός, καλός·" ἀλλ᾽ ἔτι φήσω,
   ὡς καλός, ὡς χαρίεις ὄμμασι Δωσίθεος.

CXXVII   MELEAGER

I saw Alexis strolling down the road
One noon, when Summer's locks were cropped. He glowed
So twin beams dazzled me, the sexy ones
His boyish eyes emitted, and the sun's;
But while the solar rays were quenched by night,
In dreams the form of beauty still burnt bright.
Sleep, kind to others, proved to me unkind,
Etching this incandescence in my mind.

CXXVIII   MELEAGER

No longer shall the hillsides shrill with an
Air to Daphnis flattering randy Pan;
Nor can the lyre, Apollo's mouthpiece, praise
Hyacinth garlanded with virgin bays.
Daphnis, the mountain nymphs' delight, is gone,
And Hyacinth, Apollo's paragon;
So now let Dion wield desire's baton.

CXXIX   ARATUS

The stones of Argos praise their native son,
Fair Philocles, whose far-famed name is one
Scrawled in the baths of Amphiaraus, too.
His namesake won't be worsted by a few
Inscriptions! No graffitti spread his fame,
But those who've seen him in the flesh proclaim
He outstrips anyone of the same name.

CXXX   ANONYMOUS

Again and again I've said and still repeat,
"Pretty Dositheus' eyes are sweet."

οὐ δρυός, οὐδ᾿ ἐλάτης ἐχαράξαμεν, οὐδ᾿ ἐπὶ τοίχου
τοῦτ᾿ ἔπος· ἀλλ᾿ ἐν ἐμῇ καῦσεν Ἔρως κραδίᾳ.
εἰ δέ τις οὐ φήσει, μὴ τείθεο. ναὶ μὰ σέ, δαῖμον,
ψεύδετ᾿· ἐγὼ δ᾿ ὁ λέγων τἀτρεκὲς οἶδα μόνος.

CXXXI   ΠΟΣΕΙΔΙΠΠΟΥ

Ἃ Κύπρον, ἅ τε Κύθηρα, καὶ ἃ Μίλητον ἐποιχνεῖς
καὶ καλὸν Συρίης ἱπποκρότου δάπεδον,
ἔλθοις ἵλαος Καλλιστίῳ, ἣ τὸν ἐραστὴν
οὐδέ ποτ᾿ οἰκείων ὦσεν ἀπὸ προθύρων.

CXXXII   ΜΕΛΕΑΓΡΟΥ

Οὔ σοι ταῦτ᾿ ἐβόων, ψυχή; "Ναὶ Κύπριν, ἁλώσει,
ὦ δύσερως, ἰξῷ πυκνὰ προσιπταμένη·"
οὐκ ἐβόων; εἷλέν σε πάγη. τί μάτην ἐνὶ δεσμοῖς
σπαίρεις; αὐτὸς Ἔρως τὰ πτερά σου δέδεκεν,
καὶ σ᾿ ἐπὶ πῦρ ἔστησε, μύροις δ᾿ ἔρρανε λιπόπνουν,
δῶκε δὲ διψώσῃ δάκρυα θερμὰ πιεῖν.

CXXXIIA   ΜΕΛΕΑΓΡΟΥ

Ἃ ψυχή βαρύμοχθε, σὺ δ᾿ ἄρτι μὲν ἐκ πυρὸς αἴθῃ,
ἄρτι δ᾿ ἀναψύχεις, πνεῦμ᾿ ἀναλεξαμένη.
τί κλαίεις; τὸν ἄτεγκτον ὅτ᾿ ἐν κόλποισιν Ἔρωτα
ἔτρεφες, οὐκ ᾔδεις ὡς ἐπὶ σοὶ τρέφετο;
οὐκ ᾔδεις; νῦν γνῶθι καλῶν ἄλλαγμα τροφείων,
πῦρ ἅμα καὶ ψυχρὰν δεξαμένη χιόνα.
αὐτὴ ταῦθ᾿ εἵλου· φέρε τὸν πόνον. ἄξια πάσχεις
ὧν ἔδρας, ὀπτῷ καιομένη μέλιτι.

CXXXIII   ΜΕΛΕΑΓΡΟΥ

Διψῶν ὡς ἐφίλησα θέρευς ἁπαλόχροα παῖδα,
εἶπα τότ᾿ αὐχμηρὰν δίψαν ἀποπροφυγών·

These words, inscribed upon no oak or pine
Or wall, Love branded on this heart of mine.
Believe no one who tells you otherwise;
Only I know the truth, and I'll swear he lies.

CXXXI   POSIDIPPUS

Lady who frequents Miletus, Cyprus and Cythera
And the beautiful ground of horsey Syria,
Kindly visit Callistion, the sort of whore
Who never turned a frequent visitor from her door.

CXXXII   MELEAGER

Did I not warn my soul, "You will get caught,
Flitting too often to that risky spot?"
Too late; the trap is sprung. In vain you gasp
Now Love has your pin-feathers in his grasp
And spits you on the fire, and as you sink,
Bastes you with scent, and gives you tears to drink.

CXXXII A   MELEAGER

Belaboured soul, now almost burnt to death,
And now reviving as you catch your breath,
Why weep? You took hard-hearted Love to nurse,
Never guessing he would prove a curse?
The wage of your good nursing now you know,
Receiving for it fire and frigid snow.
You asked for it, and got your just deserts,
Once burnt, apprised how Love's hot honey hurts.

CXXXIII   MELEAGER

I thirsted in the summertime to kiss
A silken lad, and, satisfied, said this:

64

"Ζεῦ πάτερ, ἆρα φίλημα τὸ νεκτάρεον Γανυμήδευς
πίνεις, καὶ τόδε σοι χείλεσιν οἰνοχοεῖ;
καὶ γὰρ ἐγὼ τὸν καλὸν ἐν ἠϊθέοισι φιλήσας
Ἀντίοχον, ψυχῆς ἡδὺ πέπωκα μέλι."

CXXXIV   ΚΑΛΛΙΜΑΧΟΥ

Ἕλκος ἔχων ὁ ξεῖνος ἐλάνθανεν· ὡς ἀνιηρὸν
πνεῦμα διὰ στηθέων, εἶδες, ἀνηγάγετο,
τὸ τρίτον ἡνίκ' ἔπινε· τὰ δὲ ῥόδα φυλλοβολεῦντα
τὠνδρὸς ἀπὸ στεφάνων πάντ' ἐγένοντο χαμαί.
ὤπτηται μέγα δή τι· μὰ δαίμονας, οὐκ ἀπὸ ῥυσμοῦ
εἰκάζω· φωρὸς δ' ἴχνια φὼρ ἔμαθον.

CXXXV   ΑΣΚΛΗΠΙΑΔΟΥ

Οἶνος ἔρωτος ἔλεγχος· ἐρᾶν ἀρνεύμενον ἡμῖν
ἤτασαν αἱ πολλαὶ Νικαγόρην προπόσεις.
καὶ γὰρ ἐδάκρυσεν καὶ ἐνύστασε, καί τι κατηφὲς
ἔβλεπε, χὠ σφιγχθεὶς οὐκ ἔμενε στέφανος.

CXXXVI   ΑΔΗΛΟΝ

Ὄρνιθες ψίθυροι, τί κεκράγατε; μή μ' ἀνιᾶτε,
τὸν τρυφερῇ παιδὸς σαρκὶ χλιαινόμενον,
ἑζόμεναι πετάλοισιν ἀηδόνες· εὗδε λάληθρον
θῆλυ γένος, δέομαι, μείνατ' ἐφ' ἡσυχίης.

CXXXVII   ΜΕΛΕΑΓΡΟΥ

Ὀρθροβόας, δυσέρωτι κακάγγελε, νῦν, τρισάλαστε,
ἐννύχιος κράζεις πλευροτυπῆ κέλαδον,
γαῦρος ὑπὲρ κοίτας, ὅτε μοι βραχὺ τοῦτ' ἔτι νυκτὸς
ζῇ τὸ φιλεῖν, ἐπ' ἐμαῖς δ' ἁδὺ γελᾷς ὀδύναις.
ἅδε φίλα θρεπτῆρι χάρις; ναὶ τὸν βαθὺν ὄρθρον,
ἔσχατα γηρύσῃ ταῦτα τὰ πικρὰ μέλη.

"Such is the kiss that Zeus like nectar sips
From Ganymede's intoxicating lips.
Kissing Antiochus, fair for his age,
My soul imbibed a honeyed beverage."

CXXXIV   CALLIMACHUS

Our quest conceals a wound we never guessed:
Look how he heaves a sigh, as if distressed,
With his third drink. The roses he was crowned
With all have shed their petals on the ground.
There's something troubling him, and my belief
Is sound: it takes a thief to catch a thief.

CXXXV   ASCLEPIADES

One test of love is wine. When he denied
His love, a glass proved Nicagoras lied:
He looked downcast, and bowed his head, and cried,
And round his brow the garland came untied.

CXXXVI   ANONYMOUS

Twittering birds, why vex me with your gabble
    While I am basking in a fleshy boy's
Charms. Go to sleep, please, nightingales, don't babble
    Among the leaves like women. Stop that noise!

CXXXVII   MELEAGER

To lovers, chanticleer, you bring bad news
    At dawn. Now when the lovelong night's so brief
Why are you making this ear-splitting noise,
    Crowing above my bed to mock my grief
Tonight? What gratitude for your upbringing!
This dawn will hear the last of your harsh singing.

CXXXVIII ΜΝΑΣΑΛΚΟΥ

Ἄμπελε, μήποτε φύλλα χαμαὶ σπεύδουσα βαλέσθαι
δείδιας ἑσπέριον Πλειάδα δυομέναν;
μεῖνον ἐπ᾽ Ἀντιλέοντι πεσεῖν ὑπὸ τὶν γλυκὺν ὕπνον,
ἐς τότε, τοῖς καλοῖς πάντα χαριζομένα.

CXXXIX ΚΑΛΛΙΜΑΧΟΥ

Ἔστι τι, ναὶ τὸν Πᾶνα, κεκρυμμένον, ἔστι τι ταύτῃ,
ναὶ μὰ Διώνυσον, πῦρ ὑπὸ τῇ σποδιῇ·
οὐ θαρσέω. μὴ δή με περίπλεκε· πολλάκι λήθει
τοῖχον ὑποτρώγων ἡσύχιος ποταμός.
τῷ καὶ νῦν δείδοικα, Μενέξενε, μή με παρεισδὺς
οὗτος ὁ †σειγαρνης εἰς τὸν ἔρωτα βάλῃ.

CXL ΑΔΗΛΟΝ

Τὸν καλὸν ὡς ἰδόμαν Ἀρχέστρατον, οὐ μὰ τὸν Ἑρμᾶν,
οὐ καλὸν αὐτὸν ἔφαν· οὐ γὰρ ἄγαν ἐδόκει.
εἶπα, καὶ ἁ Νέμεσίς με συνάρπασε, κεὐθὺς ἐκείμαν
ἐν πυρί, παῖς δ᾽ ἐπ᾽ ἐμοὶ Ζεὺς ἐκεραυνοβόλει.
τὸν παῖδ᾽ ἱλασόμεσθ᾽, ἢ τὰν θεόν; ἀλλὰ θεοῦ μοι
ἔστιν ὁ παῖς κρέσσων· χαιρέτω ἁ Νέμεσις.

CXLI ΜΕΛΕΑΓΡΟΥ

Ἐφθέγξω, ναὶ Κύπριν, ἃ μὴ θεός, ὦ μέγα τολμᾶν
θυμὲ μαθών· Θήρων σοὶ καλὸς οὐκ ἐφάνη·
σοὶ καλὸς οὐκ ἐφάνη Θήρων· ἀλλ᾽ αὐτὸς ὑπέστης,
οὐδὲ Διὸς πτήξας πῦρ τὸ κεραυνοβόλον.
τοιγάρ, ἰδού, τὸν πρόσθε λάλον προὔθηκεν ἰδέσθαι
δεῖγμα θρασυστομίης ἡ βαρύφρων Νέμεσις.

CXXXVIII   MNASALCAS

In fear of Fall, why, grapevine, do you keep
  Your leaves till the Pleiades sink in the West,
With Antileon dreamily asleep
  Beneath you? Gratify the prettiest.

CXXXIX   CALLIMACHUS

By Pan and Dionysus! there is flame
Concealed beneath these ashes all the same.
I've lost my nerve; don't hug me! Often small
Still streams unnoticed undermine a wall;
I fear the dumb insinuations of
Menexenus are prodding me to love.

CXL   ANONYMOUS

One look at Archestratus and I said,
  "His looks are not exceptional." To teach me,
Nemesis took and threw me on a bed
  Of coals, where Zeus's thunderbolts could reach me.
Which, boy or goddess, should I satisfy?
The boy is better. Nemesis, goodbye!

CXLI   MELEAGER

You uttered what no deity would dare,
Audacious critic: "Thero isn't fair."
Not fair to you, perhaps! You've no excuse,
Uncowed by all the thunderbolts of Zeus.
Grave Nemesis now ridicules your chatter
To reprimand bad manners and no matter.

68

CXLII   ΡΙΑΝΟΥ

Ἰξῷ Δεξιόνικος ὑπὸ χλωρῇ πλατανίστῳ
κόσσυφον ἀγρεύσας, εἷλε κατὰ πτερύγων·
χὠ μὲν ἀναστενάχων ἀπεκώκυεν ἱερὸς ὄρνις.
ἀλλ' ἐγώ, ὦ φίλ' Ἔρως, καὶ θαλεραὶ Χάριτες,
εἴην καὶ κίχλη καὶ κόσσυφας, ὡς ἂν ἐκείνου
ἐν χερὶ καὶ φθογγὴν καὶ γλυκὺ δάκρυ βάλω.

CXLIII   ΑΔΗΛΟΝ

Ἑρμῆ, τοξευθεὶς ἐξέσπασε πικρὸν ⟨ὀϊστὸν⟩
. . . .
. . . . ἐφήβῳ.
Κἠγὼ τὴν αὐτήν, ξεῖνε, λέλογχα τύχην.
Ἀλλά μ' Ἀπολλοφάνους τρύχει πόθος. Ὦ φιλάεθλε,
ἔφθασας· εἰς ἓν πῦρ οἱ δύ' ἐνηλάμεθα.

CXLIV   ΜΕΛΕΑΓΡΟΥ

Τί κλαίεις, φρενοληστά; τί δ' ἄγρια τόξα καὶ ἰοὺς
ἔρριψας, διφυῆ ταρσὸν ἀνεὶς πτερύγων;
ἦ ῥά γε καὶ σὲ Μυΐσκος ὁ δύσμαχος ὄμμασιν αἴθει;
ὡς μόλις οἷ ἔδρας πρόσθε παθὼν ἔμαθες.

CXLV   ΑΔΗΛΟΝ

Παύετε, παιδοφίλαι, κενεὸν πόνον· ἴσχετε μόχθων,
δύσφρονες· ἀπρήκτοις ἐλπίσι μαινόμεθα.
ἶσον ἐπὶ ψαφαρὴν ἀντλεῖν ἅλα, κἀπὸ Λιβύσσης
ψάμμου ἀριθμητὴν ἀρτιάσαι ψεκάδα,
ἶσον καὶ παίδων στέργειν πόθον, οἷς τὸ κεναυχὲς
κάλλος ἐνὶ χθονίοις ἡδύ τ' ἐν ἀθανάτοις.
δέρκεσθ' εἰς ἐμὲ πάντες· ὁ γὰρ πάρος εἰς κενὸν ἡμῶν
μόχθος ἐπὶ ξηροῖς ἐκκέχυτ' αἰγιαλοῖς.

CXLII   RHIANUS

Beneath a plane tree Dexionicus,
    Catching a blackbird, held it by the wing;
The sacred bird complained and made a fuss.
    Dear Love, you blooming Graces, let me sing
As thrush or blackbird, in that youngster's grasp
And pour forth mawkish tears at my last gasp.

CXLIII   ANONYMOUS

"Hermes, one struck by boy-love tried to pluck
The sharp barb out."
                    "I had no better luck."
"Apollophanes wastes me with desire."
"You first, we've both been thrown on the same fire."

CXLIV   MELEAGER

Thief of hearts, why jettison your cruel
    Arrows and bow and, weeping, fold your wings?
Invincible Myiscus' looks must fuel
    Repentance for your previous philanderings.

CXLV   ANONYMOUS

Unhappy paederasts, cease your inane
Exertions! All our hopes are mad. As vain
As dredging up sea-water on dry land
Or numbering the grains of desert sand
Is a yen for boys, whose indiscreet
Charms are to mortals and immortals sweet.
Just look at me! My efforts heretofore
Have all been emptied on the arid shore.

CXLVI   PIANOΥ

Ἀγρεύσας τὸν νεβρὸν ἀπώλεσα, χὠ μὲν ἀνατλὰς
μυρία, καὶ στήσας δίκτυα καὶ στάλικας,
σὺν κενεαῖς χείρεσσιν ἀπέρχομαι· οἱ δ᾽ ἀμόγητοι
τἀμὰ φέρουσιν, Ἔρως· οἷς σὺ γένοιο βαρύς.

CXLVII   ΜΕΛΕΑΓΡΟΥ

Ἅρπασται· τίς τόσσον ἐναιχμάσαι ἄγριος εἴη;
τὶς τόσος ἀντᾶραι καὶ πρὸς Ἔρωτα μάχην;
ἅπτε τάχος πεύκας. καίτοι κτύπος· Ἡλιοδώρας.
βαῖνε πάλιν στέρνων ἐντὸς ἐμῶν, κραδίη.

CXLVIII   ΚΑΛΛΙΜΑΧΟΥ

Οἶδ᾽ ὅτι μου πλούτου κενεαὶ χέρες· ἀλλά, Μένιππε,
μὴ λέγε, πρὸς Χαρίτων, τοὐμὸν ὄνειρον ἐμοί.
ἀλγέω τὴν διὰ παντὸς ἔπος τόδε πικρὸν ἀκούω
ναί, φίλε, τῶν παρὰ σοῦ τοῦτ᾽ ἀνεραστότατον.

CXLIX   ΚΑΛΛΙΜΑΧΟΥ

"Ληφθήσῃ, περίφευγε, Μενέκρατες·" εἶπα Πανήμου
εἰκάδι, καὶ Λώου τῇ—τίνι; τῇ δεκάτῃ
ἦλθεν ὁ βοῦς ὑπ᾽ ἄροτρον ἑκούσιος. εὖγ᾽ ἐμὸς Ἑρμᾶς,
εὖγ᾽ ἐμός· οὐ παρὰ τὰς εἴκοσι μεμφόμεθα.

CL   ΚΑΛΛΙΜΑΧΟΥ

Ὡς ἀγαθὰν Πολύφαμος ἀνεύρατο τὰν ἐπαοιδὰν
τὠραμένῳ· ναὶ Γᾶν, οὐκ ἀμαθὴς ὁ Κύκλωψ.
αἱ Μοῖσαι τὸν ἔρωτα κατισχναίνοντι, Φίλιππε·
ἦ πανακὲς πάντων φάρμακον ἁ σοφία.

CXLVI   RHIANUS

As soon as I had trapped I lost the kid;
    I'd staked out snares and laboured to deploy them,
But came off empty-handed. Those who did
    No work take what is mine—may Love destroy them!

CXLVII   MELEAGER

Kidnapped! Who would have the nerve to try it?
    Against Love who is so bold to campaign?
Hurry, light the lamps! A footstep? Quiet!
    My heart, get back inside my breast again!

CXLVIII   CALLIMACHUS

I know I am not wealthy, Menippus;
    Don't tell me what I perfectly recall.
I'm pained by your constant acrimonious
    Words, the most unloving thrusts of all.

CXLIX   CALLIMACHUS

Last month Menecrates, you know I joked
    You would be caught although you ran away?
This month the bull calf's eager to be yoked,
    But I shall not complain of the delay.

CL   CALLIMACHUS

How excellent the love-charm Polyphemus
Invented! That cyclops was no ignoramus.
The Muses starve desire into submission,
And wisdom is a general physician.

72

τοῦτο, δοκέω, χὰ λιμὸς ἔχει μόνον ἐς τὰ πονηρὰ
τὠγαθόν, ἐκκόπτει τὰν φιλόπαιδα νόσον.
ἔσθ' ἁμῖν χὰκαστὰς ἀφειδέα πρὸς τὸν Ἔρωτα.
τοῦτ' εἶπαι "Κείρευ τὰ πτερά, παιδάριον·
οὐδ' ὅσον ἀττάραγόν σε δεδοίκαμες"· αἱ γὰρ ἐπῳδαὶ
οἴκοι τῶ χαλεπῶ τραύματος ἀμφότεραι.

CLI   ΑΔΗΛΟΝ

Εἴ τινά που παίδων ἐρατώτατον ἄνθος ἔχοντα
εἶδες, ἀδιστάκτως εἶδες Ἀπολλόδοτον.
εἰ δ' ἐσιδών, ὦ ξεῖνε, πυριφλέκτοισι πόθοισιν
οὐκ ἐδάμης, πάντως ἢ θεὸς ἢ λίθος εἶ.

CLII   ΑΔΗΛΟΝ

Μάγνης Ἡράκλειτος, ἐμοὶ πόθος, οὔτι σίδηρον
πέτρῳ, πνεῦμα δ' ἐμὸν κάλλει ἐφελκόμενος.

CLIII   ΑΣΚΛΗΠΙΑΔΟΥ

Πρόσθε μοι Ἀρχεάδης ἐθλίβετο· νῦν δὲ τάλαιναν
οὐδ' ὅσσον παίζων εἰς ἔμ' ἐπιστρέφεται.
οὐδ' ὁ μελιχρὸς Ἔρως ἀεὶ γλυκύς· ἀλλ' ἀνιήσας
πολλάκις ἡδίων γίνετ' ἐρῶσι θεός.

CLIV   ΜΕΛΕΑΓΡΟΥ

Ἡδὺς ὁ παῖς, καὶ τοὔνομ' ἐμοὶ γλυκύς ἐστι Μυΐσκος
καὶ χαρίεις· τίν' ἔχω μὴ οὐχὶ φιλεῖν πρόφασιν;
καλὸς γάρ, ναὶ Κύπριν, ὅλος καλός· εἰ δ' ἀνιηρός,
οἶδε τὸ πικρὸν Ἔρως συγκεράσαι μέλιτι.

There's this to recommend the pangs of hunger,
Philip: they cure sick hankerings for younger
Boys. To the love god I pronounce this spell, "Oh
Ho, your wings are clipped, my little fellow!
I don't fear you one bit. At home I have,
For Love's infected wound, two kinds of salve."

CLI   ANONYMOUS

When you beheld the sexiest of blooming
      Boys, Apollodotus you were shown;
If you weren't overwhelmed by all-consuming
      Lust, a god you must be, or a stone.

CLII   ANONYMOUS

Attractive Heraclitus is my own
Magnet, not drawing iron like a stone,
But my soul by his loveliness alone.

CLIII   ASCLEPIADES

Once Archeades used to rub against
      Me, now when playing games he doesn't nod.
Love's not all honeydew. When he torments
      Us Love becomes an even sweeter god.

CLIV   MELEAGER

Myiscus' name is charming, too, which leaves me
      No reason for not falling at his feet.
He's beautiful all over. When he grieves me,
      Love interweaves the bitter with the sweet.

74

CLV ΑΔΗΛΟΝ

α. Μή μ' εἴπῃς πάλιν ὦδε. β. Τί δ' αἴτιος; αὐτὸς ἔπεμψε.
α. Δεύτερον οὖν φήσεις; β. Δεύτερον. εἶπεν· Ἴθι.
ἀλλ' ἔρχευ, μὴ μέλλε. μένουσί σε. α. Πρῶτον ἐκείνους
εὑρήσω, χἤξω· τὸ τρίτον οἶδα πάλαι.

CLVI ΑΔΗΛΟΝ

Εἰαρινῷ χειμῶνι πανείκελος, ὦ Διόδωρε,
οὑμὸς ἔρως, ἀσαφεῖ κρινόμενος πελάγει·
καὶ ποτὲ μὲν φαίνεις πολὺν ὑετόν, ἄλλοτε δ' αὖτε
εὔδιος, ἁβρὰ γελῶν δ' ὄμμασιν ἐκκέχυσαι.
τυφλὰ δ', ὅπως ναυηγὸς ἐν οἴδματι, κύματα μετρῶν
δινεῦμαι, μεγάλῳ χείματι πλαζόμενος.
ἀλλά μοι ἢ φιλίης ἔκθες σκοπὸν ἢ πάλι μίσους,
ὡς εἰδῶ ποτέρῳ κύματι νηχόμεθα.

CLVII ΜΕΛΕΑΓΡΟΥ

Κύπρις ἐμοὶ ναύκληρος, Ἔρως δ' οἴακα φυλάσσει
ἄκρον ἔχων ψυχῆς ἐν χερὶ πηδάλιον·
χειμαίνει δ' ὁ βαρὺς πνεύσας Πόθος, οὕνεκα δὴ νῦν
παμφύλῳ παίδων νήχομαι ἐν πελάγει.

CLVIII ΜΕΛΕΑΓΡΟΥ

Σοί με Πόθων δέσποινα θεὴ πόρε, σοί με, Θεόκλεις,
ἁβροπέδιλος Ἔρως γυμνὸν ὑπεστόρεσεν,
ξεῖνον ἐπὶ ξείνης, δαμάσας ἀλύτοισι χαλινοῖς·
ἱμείρω δὲ τυχεῖν ἀκλινέος φιλίας.

CLV   ANONYMOUS

[Boy] Don't speak to me like that again!

                              [Go-between] No, no,

Only someone sent me . . . Don't be vexed.

[Boy] That's the second time!

                          [Go-between] He told me, 'Go!'

Come on, they're waiting for you. Why so slow?

[Boy] We'll see who's waiting. I know what comes next.

CLVI   ANONYMOUS

My love, Diodorus, is like a spring
Storm, of the fluid sea's engendering.
You imitate a thundercloud, then after
The weather clears, your eyes brim with soft laughter.
Like a castaway who counts the steep
Waves, I am tempest-tossed upon the deep;
Give me, that I may know in which direction
To swim, marks of aversion or affection.

CLVII   MELEAGER

My skipper's Venus, Cupid mans the helm,
     Holding my spirit's rudder in his hand;
Desire blows hard enough to overwhelm
     Me, breasting a sea of boys from every land.

CLVIII   MELEAGER

To you, Theocles, Mistress Venus gave
Me. Stretched out at your feet, a naked slave,
An outcast, I was tamed by Love's tight grip.
I'd like a less abject relationship,

άλλά σύ τον στέργοντ᾽ άπαναίνεαι, ουδέ σε θέλγει
ού χρόνος, ου ξυνής σύμβολα σωφροσύνης.
ίλαθ᾽, άναξ, ίληθι· σε γαρ θεον ώρισε Δαίμων·
εν σοί μοι ζωής πείρατα και θανάτου.

CLIX   ΜΕΛΕΑΓΡΟΥ

Εν σοὶ τἀμά, Μυΐσκε, βίου πρυμνήσι᾽ ανήπται·
εν σοὶ καὶ ψυχής πνεύμα το λειφθεν ετι.
ναὶ γαρ δη τα σά, κούρε, τα καὶ κωφοίσι λαλεύντα
όμματα, καὶ μα το σον φαιδρον επισκύνιον,
ήν μοι συννεφες όμμα βάλης ποτέ, χείμα δέδορκα·
ήν δ᾽ ιλαρον βλέψης, ηδυ τέθηλεν εαρ.

CLX   ΑΔΗΛΟΝ

Θαρσαλέως τρηχείαν υπο σπλάγχνοισιν ανίην
οίσω, καὶ χαλεπής δεσμον αλυκτοπέδης.
ου γαρ πω, Νίκανδρε, βολας εδάημεν Έρωτος
νύν μόνον, αλλα πόθων πολλάκις ηψάμεθα.
καὶ σύ μέν, Άδρήστεια, κακής ανταξια βουλής
τίσαι, καὶ μακάρων πικροτάτη Νέμεσις.

CLXI   ΑΣΚΛΗΠΙΑΔΟΥ

Δόρκιον η φιλέφηβος επίσταται, ως απαλος παίς,
έσθαι πανδήμου Κύπριδος ωκυ βέλος,
ίμερον αστράπτουσα κατ᾽ όμματος, ηδ᾽ υπερ ώμων
....
....
συν πετάσω γυμνον μηρον έφαινε χλαμύς.

But you rebuff my overtures, unmoved
By how far our relations have improved.
Have pity, lord! For god made you divine:
The means of life and death are yours, not mine.

CLIX   MELEAGER

To you, Myiscus, my whole soul is tied,
And all the life and breath in me beside,
For by your eyes that speak, I don't know how,
To deaf and dumb, and by your shining brow,
Your gloomy glance or laughing look can bring
The chill of winter or the flowers of spring.

CLX   ANONYMOUS

Bravely shall I endure my inner pain,
The bondage of this irritating chain;
It's not the first time I have learned Love's ire,
Nicander: often have I felt desire.
May Nemesis exact harsh recompense,
Implacably, for his malevolence.

CLXI   ASCLEPIADES

Youth-loving Dorcion knows how to shoot
    Swift darts of vulgar Venus from her eyes,
Dazzling with desire, just like some cute
    Boy with his cap and smock and naked thighs.

78

CLXII ΑΣΚΛΗΠΙΑΔΟΥ

Οὔπω τοξοφορῶν οὐδ᾽ ἄγριος, ἀλλὰ νεογνὸς
οὑμὸς Ἔρως παρὰ τὴν Κύπριν ὑποστρέφεται,
δέλτον ἔχων χρυσέην· τὰ Φιλοκράτεος δὲ Διαύλου
τραυλίζει ψυχῆς φίλτρα κατ᾽ Ἀντιγένους.

CLXIII ΑΣΚΛΗΠΙΑΔΟΥ

Εὗρεν Ἔρως τὶ καλῷ μίξει καλόν, οὐχὶ μάραγδον
χρυσῷ, ὃ μήτ᾽ ἀνθεῖ, μήτε γένοιτ᾽ ἐν ἴσῳ,
οὐδ᾽ ἐλέφαντ᾽ ἐβένῳ, λευκῷ μέλαν, ἀλλὰ Κλέανδρον
Εὐβιότῳ, Πειθοῦς ἄνθεα καὶ Φιλίης.

CLXIV ΜΕΛΕΑΓΡΟΥ

Ἡδὺ μὲν ἀκρήτῳ κεράσαι γλυκὺ νᾶμα μελισσῶν·
ἡδὺ δὲ παιδοφιλεῖ καὐτὸν ἐόντα καλόν,
οἷα τὸν ἁβροκόμην στέργει Κλεόβουλον Ἄλεξις·
ἀθάνατον τούτῳ Κύπριδος οἰνόμελι.

CLXV ΜΕΛΕΑΓΡΟΥ

Λευκανθὴς Κλεόβουλος· ὁ δ᾽ ἀντία τοῦδε μελίχρους
Σώπολις, οἱ δισσοὶ Κύπριδος ἀνθοφόροι.
τοὔνεκά μοι παίδων ἕπεται πόθος· οἱ γὰρ Ἔρωτες
ἐκ λευκοῦ πλέξαι φασί με καὶ μέλανος.

CLXVI ΑΣΚΛΗΠΙΑΔΟΥ

Τοῦθ᾽ ὅ τί μοι λοιπὸν ψυχῆς, ὅ τι δή ποτ᾽, Ἔρωτες,
τοῦτό γ᾽ ἔχειν πρὸς θεῶν ἡσυχίην ἄφετε·
ἢ μὴ δὴ τόξοις ἔτι βάλλετέ μ᾽, ἀλλὰ κεραυνοῖς·
ναὶ πάντως τέφρην θέσθε με κἀνθρακιήν.
ναί, ναί, βάλλετ᾽, Ἔρωτες· ἐνεσκληκὼς γὰρ ἀνίαις,
ἐξ ὑμέων τοῦτ᾽ οὖν, εἴ γέ τι, βούλομ᾽ ἔχειν.

CLXII   ASCLEPIADES

While not yet armed and dangerous, my love,
      An infant, comes to Venus holding these
Tablets of gold, and lisps the love-charms of
      Philocrates that psyched Antigenes.

CLXIII   ASCLEPIADES

Love has devised a winning combination—
      Not emerald with gold, which glitters less,
Nor ebony with ivory. Solicitation
      Shows Eubolus Cleander's friendliness.

CLXIV   MELEAGER

Honey-flavoured wine's as savorous
      As boy-love when oneself is under-age.
Alexis' love for sleek Cleobulus
      Is Venus' sweet, immortal beverage.

CLXV   MELEAGER

Cleobulus' candid blossoms opposite
      Sopolis' honey-coloured bloom excite
Lust for these flower-boys. They say Love knit
      Me, Meleager, out of black and white.

CLXVI   ASCLEPIADES

If of my soul there's still some tiny piece
Left, Loves, please do let it rest in peace,
Or, not with arrows but with lightning-flashes,
Reduce me totally to smoking ashes.
Yes, strike me down, exhausted and distressed:
Grant me, if nothing more, this last request.

CLXVII   ΜΕΛΕΑΓΡΟΥ

Χειμέριον μὲν πνεῦμα· φέρει δ' ἐπὶ σοί με, Μυΐσκε,
ἁρπαστὸν κώμοις ὁ γλυκύδακρυς Ἔρως.
χειμαίνει δὲ βαρὺς πνεύσας Πόθος, ἀλλά μ' ἐς ὅρμον
δέξαι, τὸν ναύτην Κύπριδος ἐν πελάγει.

CLXVIII   ΠΟΣΕΙΔΙΠΠΟΥ

Ναννοῦς καὶ Λύδης ἐπίχει δύο, καὶ φιλεράστου
Μιμνέρμου, καὶ τοῦ σώφρονος Ἀντιμάχου·
συγκέρασον τὸν πέμπτον ἐμοῦ· τὸν δ' ἕκτον ἑκάστου,
Ἡλιόδωρ', εἶπας, ὅστις ἐρῶν ἔτυχεν·
ἕβδομον Ἡσιόδου, τὸν δ' ὄγδοον εἶπον Ὁμήρου,
τὸν δ' ἔνατον Μουσῶν, Μνημοσύνης δέκατον.
μεστὸν ὑπὲρ χείλους πίομαι, Κύπρι· τἆλλα δ' Ἔρωτες
νήφοντ' οἰνωθέντ' οὐχὶ λίην ἄχαριν.

CLXIX   ΔΙΟΣΚΟΡΙΔΟΥ

Ἐξέφυγον, Θεόδωρε, τὸ σὸν βάρος. ἀλλ' ὅσον εἶπας
"Ἐξέφυγον τὸν ἐμὸν δαίμονα πικρότατον,"
πικρότερός με κατέσχεν. Ἀριστοκράτει δὲ λατρεύων
μυρία, δεσπόσυνον καὶ τρίτον ἐκδέχομαι.

CLXX   ΔΙΟΣΚΟΡΙΔΟΥ

Σπονδὴ καὶ λιβανωτέ, καὶ οἱ κρητῆρι μιγέντες
δαίμονες, οἳ φιλίης τέρματ' ἐμῆς ἔχετε,
ὑμέας, ὦ σεμνοί, μαρτύρομαι, οὓς ὁ μελίχρως
κοῦρος Ἀθήναιος πάντας ἐπωμόσατο.

81

CLXVII   MELEAGER

Myiscus, despite this wintry wind I'm swept
    Away by Love's sweet tears to pay you court.
Desire is like a hurricane. Accept
    This loving mariner into your port.

CLXVIII   POSIDIPPUS

To Nanno and to Lydé, that makes two
Cups; to Mimnermus, sympathetic to
Lovers, and prudish Antimachus too.
The fifth's for me, the sixth in honour of
Anyone who ever fell in love.
Hesiod, seven, Homer, eight, and then
The Muses, nine, and Memory makes ten.
I drain the brimming bowl to Love, a lad
Who, drunk or sober, doesn't look too bad.

CLXIX   DIOSCORIDES

I thought I had escaped my worst oppressor,
    Theodore, when I threw off your weight.
Aristocrates proved a worse successor,
    And now my third slavemaster I await.

CLXX   DIOSCORIDES

By frankincense and by libations I
    Swear, and the potations that decide
The limits of our friendship, dread gods by
    Whom dusky Athenaeus testified.

CLXXI   ΔΙΟΣΚΟΡΙΔΟΥ

Τὸν καλόν, ὡς ἔλαβες, κομίσαις πάλιπρός με θεωρὸν
Εὐφραγόρην, ἀνέμων πρηΰτατε Ζέφυρε,
εἰς ὀλίγων τείνας μηνῶν μέτρον· ὡς καὶ ὁ μικρὸς
μυριετὴς κέκριται τῷ φιλέοντι χρόνος.

CLXXII   ΕΥΗΝΟΥ

Εἰ μισεῖν πόνος ἐστί, φιλεῖν πόνος, ἐκ δύο λυγρῶν
αἱροῦμαι χρηστῆς ἕλκος ἔχειν ὀδύνης.

CLXXIII   ΦΙΛΟΔΗΜΟΥ

Δημώ με κτείνει καὶ Θέρμιον· ἡ μὲν ἑταίρη,
Δημονόη δ᾽ οὔπω Κύπριν ἐπισταμένη.
καὶ τῆς μὲν ψαύω· τῆς δ᾽ οὐ θέμις. οὐ μὰ σέ, Κύπρι,
οὐκ οἶδ᾽ ἣν εἰπεῖν δεῖ με ποθεινοτέρην.
Δημάριον λέξω τὴν παρθένον· οὐ γὰρ ἕτοιμα
βούλομαι, ἀλλὰ ποθῶ πᾶν τὸ φυλασσόμενον.

CLXXIV   ΦΡΟΝΤΩΝΟΣ

Μέχρι τίνος πολεμεῖς μ᾽, ὦ φίλτατε Κῦρε; τί ποιεῖς;
τὸν σὸν Καμβύσην οὐκ ἐλεεῖς; λέγε μοι.
μὴ γίνου Μῆδος· Σάκας γὰρ ἔσῃ μετὰ μικρόν,
καὶ σε ποιήσουσιν ταὶ τρίχες Ἀστυάγην.

CLXXV   ΣΤΡΑΤΩΝΟΣ

Ἢ μὴ ζηλοτύπει δούλοις ἐπὶ παισὶν ἑταίρους,
ἢ μὴ θηλυπρεπεῖς οἰνοχόους πάρεχε.
τίς γὰρ ἀνὴρ ἐς ἔρωτ᾽ ἀδαμάντινος; ἢ τίς ἀτειρὴς
οἴνῳ; τίς δὲ καλοὺς οὐ περίεργα βλέπει;
ζώντων ἔργα τάδ᾽ ἐστίν· ὅπου δ᾽ οὐκ εἰσὶν ἔρωτες
οὐδὲ μέθαι, Διοφῶν, ἢν ἐθέλῃς, ἄπιθι·

CLXXI   DIOSCORIDES

Zephyr, bring beautiful Euphragoras
    Back, whom you took away not long ago
On pilgrimage. For lovers short months pass
    Like a milenium, but twice as slow.

CLXXII   EVENUS

Since hating's a bore and loving is a bore,
I like the nicer of two boredoms more.

CLXXIII   PHILODEMUS

Demo and Thermion slay me: one's a whore
Whereas the other doesn't know the score.
I fondle one, the other I may not;
I don't know which one I desire more!
The virgin, I'll say; for I don't long for what
Is handy, but what is arduously got.

CLXXIV   FRONTO

How much longer, Cyrus, will you fight us
    Off? You should be nice to older men.
Soon you'll get Harry, so do not play Titus
    Now, for you will not be stuck-up then.

CLXXV   STRATO

If you don't want your cronies leering at
Your slaveboys, pick them less effeminate.
What man of adamant resists the joys
Of love and wine and quizzing pretty boys?
They're part of living. But to some place with no
Drinking or sex, if that's your crotchet, go:

κἀκεῖ Τειρεσίην ἢ Τάνταλον ἐς πότον ἕλκε,
τὸν μὲν ἐπ᾽ οὐδὲν ἰδεῖν, τὸν δ᾽ ἐπὶ μοῦνον ἰδεῖν.

CLXXVI   ΣΤΡΑΤΩΝΟΣ

Στυγνὸς δὴ τί, Μένιππε, κατεσκέπασαι μέχρι πέζης,
ὁ πρὶν ἐπ᾽ ἰγνύης λῶπος ἀνελκόμενος;
ἢ τί κάτω κύψας με παρέδραμες, οὐδὲ προσειπών;
οἶδα τί με κρύπτεις· ἤλυθον ἃς ἔλεγον.

CLXXVII   ΣΤΡΑΤΩΝΟΣ

Ἑσπερίην Μοῖρίς με, καθ᾽ ἣν ὑγιαίνομεν ὥρην,
οὐκ οἶδ᾽ εἴτε σαφῶς, εἴτ᾽ ὄναρ, ἠσπάσατο.
ἤδη γὰρ τὰ μὲν ἄλλα μάλ᾽ ἀτρεκέως ἐνόησα,
χὠκόσα μοι προσέφη, χὠκόσ᾽ ἐπυνθάνετο·
εἰ δέ με καὶ πεφίληκε τεκμαίρομαι· εἰ γὰρ ἀληθές,
πῶς ἀποθειωθεὶς πλάζομ᾽ ἐπιχθόνιος;

CLXXVIII   ΣΤΡΑΤΩΝΟΣ

Ἐξεφλέγην, ὅτε Θεῦδις ἐλάμπετο παισὶν ἐν ἄλλοις,
οἷος ἐπαντέλλων ἀστράσιν ἠέλιος.
τοὔνεκ᾽ ἔτι φλέγομαι καὶ νῦν, ὅτε νυκτὶ λαχνοῦται·
δυόμενος γάρ, ὅμως ἥλιός ἐστιν ἔτι.

CLXXIX   ΣΤΡΑΤΩΝΟΣ

Ὤμοσά σοι, Κρονίδη, μηπώποτε, μηδ᾽ ἐμοὶ αὐτῷ
ἐξειπεῖν ὅ τι μοι Θεῦδις ἔειπε λαβεῖν.
ψυχὴ δ᾽ ἡ δυσάπιστος ἀγαλλομένη πεπότηται
ἠέρι, καὶ στέξαι τἀγαθὸν οὐ δύναται·
ἀλλ᾽ ἐρέω, σύγγνωθι σύ μοι, κεῖνος δὲ πέπεισται.
Ζεῦ πάτερ, ἀγνώστου τίς χάρις εὐτυχίης;

Tiresias and Tantalus meet there,
One cannot see, and one can only stare.

CLXXVI   STRATO

Menippus, why go shrouded to your feet?
      You used to hike your robe up to your thighs.
Why hang your head in silence when we meet?
      Your prickly privates come as no surprise.

CLXXVII   STRATO

Last night Moiris, when we said goodnight—
Really, or was I dreaming?—squeezed me tight.
Everything else I perfectly recall,
What he asked me, what he said, and all.
I guess he kissed me; but, if that is so,
Why, raised to heaven, linger here below?

CLXXVIII   STRATO

Theudnis turned me on, all other bright
      Stellar boys his rising sun outshone;
He's still a sun, though in decline: each night
      More hirsute, nonetheless he turns me on.

CLXXIX   STRATO

I swore I'd never tell a soul a thing
(Not even myself) of Theudnis' offering.
But my rebellious soul could not refuse
In exultation spreading the good news.
In a word—forgive me—he put out.
What use is luck you cannot brag about?

CLXXX ΣΤΡΑΤΩΝΟΣ

Καῦμά μ᾿ ἔχει μέγα δή τι· σὺ δ᾿, ὦ παῖ, παύεο λεπτὸν
ἠέρι δινεύων ἐγγὺς ἐμεῖο λίνον.
ἄλλο τι πῦρ ἐμοῦ ἔνδον ἔχω κυάθοισιν ἀναφθέν,
καὶ περὶ σῇ ῥιπῇ μᾶλλον ἐγειρόμενον.

CLXXXI ΣΤΡΑΤΩΝΟΣ

Ψευδέα μυθίζουσι, Θεόκλεες, ὡς ἀγαθαὶ μὲν
αἱ Χάριτες, τρισσαὶ δ᾿ εἰσὶ κατ᾿ Ὀρχομενόν·
πεντάκι γὰρ δέκα σεῖο περισκιρτῶσι πρόσωπα,
τοξοβόλοι, ψυχέων ἅρπαγες ἀλλοτρίων.

CLXXXII ΣΤΡΑΤΩΝΟΣ

Ταῦτά με νῦν τὰ περισσὰ φιλεῖς, ὅτ᾿ ἔρωτος ἀπέσβη
πυρσός, ὅτ᾿ οὐδ᾿ ἄλλως ἡδὺν ἔχω σε φίλον.
μέμνημαι γὰρ ἐκεῖνα τὰ δύσμαχα· πλὴν ἔτι, Δάφνι,
ὀψὲ μέν, ἀλλ᾿ ἐχέτω καὶ μετάνο α τόπον.

CLXXXIII ΣΤΡΑΤΩΝΟΣ

Τίς χάρις, Ἡλιόδωρε, φιλήμασιν, εἴ με λάβροισιν
χείλεσι μὴ φιλέεις ἀντιβιαζόμενος,
ἀλλ᾿ ἐπ᾿ ἄκροις ἀσάλευτα μεμυκόσιν, οἷα κατ᾿ οἴκους
καὶ δίχα σοῦ με φιλεῖ πλάσμα τὸ κηρόχυτον;

CLXXXIV ΣΤΡΑΤΩΝΟΣ

Μὴ σπεύσῃς Μενέδημον ἑλεῖν δόλῳ, ἀλλ᾿ ἐπίνευσον
ὀφρύσι, καὶ φανερῶς αὐτὸς ἐρεῖ· "Πρόαγε."
οὐ γὰρ ἀνάβλησις· φθάνει δέ τε καὶ τὸν ἄγοντα·
οὐδ᾿ ἀμάρης, ποταμοῦ δ᾿ ἐστὶν ἑτοιμότερος.

CLXXX   STRATO

I feel a trifle warm. You with the fine
    Napkin, boy, stop waving it about.
The fire in me was kindled by the wine
    You served; your fanning will not put it out.

CLXXXI   STRATO

It is a pious fable that the Graces
    Number three, Theocles, and are kind;
How many graceful marksmen guard your face's
    Graces, the soul-destroyers of mankind?

CLXXXII   STRATO

Don't waste your kisses, Daphnis! Love's last ember
    Is quenched, and I shall call you my sweetheart
No longer. Your resistance I remember:
    Is it too late now for a change of heart?

CLXXXIII   STRATO

Heliodorus, what's a kiss unless
    With avid lips you thrust yourself on me?
Instead you peck my cheek, emotionless,
    As if you were a waxen effigy.

CLXXXIV   STRATO

With Menedemus all you need to do
    Is wink; he'll tell you plainly, "Go ahead!"
Without demur. He's way ahead of you,
    Wide open as a ditch—or riverbed?

88

CLXXXV ΣΤΡΑΤΩΝΟΣ

Τοὺς σοβαροὺς τούτους καὶ τοὺς περιπορφυροσήμους
παῖδας, ὅσους ἡμεῖς οὐ προσεφιέμεθα,
ὥσπερ σῦκα πέτραισιν ἐπ᾽ ἀκρολόφοισι πέπειρα
ἔσθουσιν γῦπες, Δίφιλε, καὶ κόρακες.

CLXXXVI ΣΤΡΑΤΩΝΟΣ

Ἄχρι τίνος ταύτην τὴν ὀφρύα τὴν ὑπεροπτον,
Μέντορ, τηρήσεις, μηδὲ τὸ χαῖρε λέγων,
ὡς μέλλων αἰῶνα μένειν νέος, ἢ διὰ παντὸς
ὀρχεῖσθαι πυρίχην; καὶ τὸ τέλος πρόβλεπε.
ἥξει σοι πώγων, κακὸν ἔσχατον, ἀλλὰ μέγιστον·
καὶ τότ᾽ ἐπιγνώσῃ τί σπάνις ἐστὶ φίλων.

CLXXXVII ΣΤΡΑΤΩΝΟΣ

Πῶς ἀναγινώσκειν, Διονύσιε, παῖδα διδάξεις,
μηδὲ μετεκβῆναι φθόγγον ἐπιστάμενος;
ἐκ νήτης μετέβης οὕτως ταχὺς εἰς βαρύχορδον
φθόγγον, ἀπ᾽ ἰσχνοτάτης εἰς τάσιν ὀγκοτάτην.
πλὴν οὐ βασκαίνω· μελέτα μόνον· ἀμφοτέρους δὲ
κρούων, τοῖς φθονεροῖς Λάμβδα καὶ Ἄλφα λέγε.

CLXXXVIII ΣΤΡΑΤΩΝΟΣ

Εἴ σε φιλῶν ἀδικῶ καὶ τοῦτο δοκεῖς ὕβριν εἶναι,
τὴν αὐτὴν κόλασιν καὶ σὺ φίλει με λαβών.

CLXXXIX ΣΤΡΑΤΩΝΟΣ

Τίς σε κατεστεφάνωσε ῥόδοις ὅλον; εἰ μὲν ἐραστής,
ἃ μάκαρ· εἰ δ᾽ ὁ πατήρ, ὄμματα καὐτὸς ἔχει.

CLXXXV   STRATO

Such airy-fairy boys, with purple edges
    On their robes, are hard to get as those
Ripe figs that grow high up on rocky ledges,
    Which vultures gobble, Diphilus, and crows.

CLXXXVI   STRATO

Mentor, how long will you continue so
Conceited you won't even say hello,
Proposing in the Pyrrhic dance to spend
An endless youth? Look rather to your end.
Face hair will cause you terminal distress;
You'll learn the meaning, then, of friendlessness.

CLXXXVII   STRATO

How teach a boy that fundamental skill,
Sight-reading, when your voice is changing still?
From shrill soprano to gruff bass you swoop
So quickly, from a whisper to a whoop.
But study harder, show the envious
Active and passive, Dionysius.

CLXXXVIII   STRATO

If when I kiss you you consider this
Outrageous, make my penalty a kiss.

CLXXXIX   STRATO

Who crowned you with this rosy wreath? Some kind
Admirer? Your father? Well, he isn't blind.

90

CXC ΣΤΡΑΤΩΝΟΣ

Ὄλβιος ὁ γράψας σε, καὶ ὄλβιος οὗτος ὁ κάλλει
τῷ σῷ νικᾶσθαι κηρὸς ἐπιστάμενος.
θριπὸς ἐγὼ καὶ σύρμα τερηδόνος εἴθε γενοίμην,
ὡς ἀναπηδήσας τὰ ξύλα ταῦτα φάγω.

CXCI ΣΤΡΑΤΩΝΟΣ

Οὐκ ἐχθὲς παῖς ἦσθα; καὶ οὐδ' ὄναρ οὗτος ὁ πώγων
ἤλυθε· πῶς ἀνέβη τοῦτο τὸ δαιμόνιον,
καὶ τριχὶ πάντ' ἐκάλυψε τὰ πρὶν καλά; φεῦ, τί τὸ φαῦμα;
ἐχθὲς Τρωΐλος ὤν, πῶς ἐγένου Πρίαμος;

CXCII ΣΤΡΑΤΩΝΟΣ

Οὐ τέρπουσι κόμαι με, περισσότεροί τε κίκιννοι,
τέχνης, οὐ φύσεως ἔργα διδασκόμενοι·
ἀλλὰ παλαιστρίτου παιδὸς ῥύπος ὁ ψαφαρίτης,
καὶ χροιὴ μελέων σαρκὶ λιπαινομένη.
ἡδὺς ἀκαλλώπιστος ἐμὸς πόθος· ἡ δὲ γοῆτις
μορφὴ θηλυτέρης ἔργον ἔχει Παφίης.

CXCIII ΣΤΡΑΤΩΝΟΣ

Οὐδὲ Σμυρναῖαι Νεμέσεις ὅ τι σοὶ 'πιλέγουσιν,
Ἀρτεμίδωρε, νοεῖς· "Μηδὲν ὑπὲρ τὸ μέτρον."
ἀλλ' οὕτως ὑπέροπτα καὶ ἄγρια κοὐδὲ πρέποντα
κωμῳδῷ φθέγγῃ, πάνθ' ὑποκρινόμενος.
μνησθήσῃ τούτων, ὑπερήφανε· καὶ σὺ φιλήσεις,
καὶ κωμῳδήσεις τὴν Ἀποκλειομένην.

CXCIV ΣΤΡΑΤΩΝΟΣ

Εἰ Ζεὺς ἐκ γαίης θνητοὺς ἔτι παῖδας ἐς αἴθρην
ἥρπαζεν, γλυκεροῦ νέκταρος οἰνοχόους,

CXC   STRATO

Happy the artist and the medium
Which by your loveliness were overcome!
I wish I were a woodworm, feeding on
The board on which your likeness has been drawn.

CXCI   STRATO

Just yesterday a boy, till this damned beard,
    Undreamt of, suddenly appeared somehow,
Hiding with hair your former beauty. Weird
    How one who was Troilus then is Priam now!

CXCII   STRATO

Long hair, abundant artificial curls
Give me no pleasure: they belong on girls.
No, give me boys all sweaty from the gym,
Glistening with oil on every limb.
I like sex unembellished, scenting in
Glamour a whiff of something feminine.

CXCIII   STRATO

Ignoring Nemesis, whose strictures stress,
Artemidorus, "Nothing in excess",
You act more arrogant and boorish than
The most uncouth, loud-mouthed comedian.
Remember this, proud lad, when you are crossed
In love, and must perform *Love's Labour's Lost*.

CXCIV   STRATO

If Zeus still snatched up mortal boys on high
To serve delicious nectar in the sky,

92

αἰετὸς ἂν πτερύγεσσιν Ἀγρίππαν τὸν καλὸν ἡμῶν
ἤδη πρὸς μακάρων ἦγε διηκονίας.
ναὶ μὰ σὲ γάρ, Κρονίδη, κόσμου πάτερ, ἢν ἐσα-θρήσῃς,
τὸν Φρύγιον ψέξεις αὐτίκα Δαρδανίδην.

CXCV   ΣΤΡΑΤΩΝΟΣ

Ἄνθεσιν οὐ τόσσοισι φιλοζέφυροι χλοάουσι
λειμῶνες, πυκιναῖς εἴαρος ἀγλαΐαις,
ὅσσους εὐγενέτας, Διονύσιε, παῖδας ἀθρήσεις,
χειρῶν Κυπρογενοῦς πλάσματα καὶ Χαρίτων.
ἔξοχα δ᾽ ἐν τούτοις Μιλήσιος ἠνίδε θάλλει,
ὡς ῥόδον εὐόδμοις λαμπόμενον πετάλοις.
ἀλλ᾽ οὐκ οἶδεν ἴσως, ἐκ καύματος ὡς καλὸν ἄνθος,
οὕτω τὴν ὥρην ἐκ τριχὸς ὀλλυμένην.

CXCVI   ΣΤΡΑΤΩΝΟΣ

Ὀφθαλμοὺς σπινθῆρας ἔχεις, φεόμορφε Λυκῖνε,
μᾶλλον δ᾽ ἀκτῖνας, δέσποτα, πυρσοβόλους.
ἀντωπὸς βλέψαι βαιὸν χρόνον οὐ δύναμαί σοι·
οὕτως ἀστράπτεις ὄμμασιν ἀμφοτέροις.

CXCVII   ΣΤΡΑΤΩΝΟΣ

"Καιρὸν γνῶθι" σοφῶν τῶν ἑπτά τις, εἶπε, Φίλιππε·
πάντα γὰρ ἀκμάζοντ᾽ ἐστὶν ἐραστότερα·
καὶ σίκυος πρῶτός που ἐπ᾽ ἀνδήροισιν ὁραθεὶς
τίμιος, εἶτα συῶν βρῶμα πεπαινόμενος.

CXCVIII   ΣΤΡΑΤΩΝΟΣ

Ἡλικίης φίλος εἰμὶ καὶ οὐδένα παῖδα προτάσσω,
πρὸς τὸ· καλὸν κρίνων· ἄλλο γὰρ ἄλλος ἔχει.

By now a pinioned eagle would have pressed
My darling into service with the blest.
But let the ruler of the world take heed:
Agrippa will eclipse his Ganymede.

CXCV   STRATO

There are no breezy meadows blossoming
So densely with the splendours of the spring
As, Dionysius, you'll see acclaimed
Boys here by Venus and the Graces framed.
Milesius, outstanding among those,
Flourishes like a fragrant, lustrous rose,
Oblivious, perhaps, that as a fair
Flower wilts in the heat, his prime hangs by a hair.

CXCVI   STRATO

Your sparkling eyes, Lycinus, what divine
        Beauties! Call them rather fiery rays.
I cannot, facing you, sustain with mine
        Momentarily your blazing gaze.

CXCVII   STRATO

Which of the sages said, "Know the right time,"
Philip? All things are choicest at their prime.
A green cucumber is praiseworthy till
Overripe, when it becomes pig swill.

CXCVIII   STRATO

A friend of youth, I have no youth in mind,
For each has beauties, of a different kind.

CXCIX ΣΤΡΑΤΩΝΟΣ

Ἄρκιον ἤδη μοι πόσιος μέτρον· εὐσταθίη γὰρ
λύεται ἤ τε φρενῶν ἤ τε διὰ στόματος.
χὠ λύχνος ἔσχισται διδύμην φλόγα, καὶ δὶς ἀριθμέω,
πολλάκι πειράζων, τοὺς ἀνακεκλιμένους.
ἤδη δ᾽ οὐκέτι μοῦνον ἐπ᾽ οἰνοχόον σεσόβημαι,
ἀλλὰ πάρωρα βλέπω κἠπὶ τὸν ὑδροχόον.

CC ΣΤΡΑΤΩΝΟΣ

Μισῶ δυσπερίληπτα φιλήματα, καὶ μαχιμώδεις
φωνάς, καὶ σθεναρὴν ἐκ χερὸς ἀντίθεσιν·
καὶ μὴν καὶ τόν, ὅτ᾽ ἐστὶν ἐν ἀγκάσιν, εὐθὺ θέλοντα
καὶ παρέχοντα χύδην, οὐ πάνυ δή τι θέλω·
ἀλλὰ τὸν ἐκ τούτων ἀμφοῖν μέσον, οἷον ἐκεῖνον
τὸν καὶ μὴ παρέχειν εἰδότα καὶ παρέχειν.

CCI ΣΤΡΑΤΩΝΟΣ

Εἰ μὴ νῦν Κλεόνικος ἐλεύσεται, οὐκέτ᾽ ἐκεῖνον
δέξομ᾽ ἐγὼ μελάθροις, οὐ μὰ τὸν—οὐκ ὀμόσω.
εἰ γὰρ ὄνειρον ἰδὼν οὐκ ἤλυθεν, εἶτα παρείη
αὔριον, οὐ παρὰ τὴν σήμερον ὀλλύμεθα.

CCII ΣΤΡΑΤΩΝΟΣ

Πτηνὸς Ἔρως ἄγαγέν με δι᾽ ἠέρος, ἡνίκα, Δᾶμι,
γράμμα σὸν εἶδον, ὅ μοι δεῦρο μολεῖν σ᾽ ἔλεγεν·
ῥίμφα δ᾽ ἀπὸ Σμύρνης ἐπὶ Σάρδιας· ἔδραμεν ἄν μοι
ὕστερον εἰ Ζήτης ἔτρεχεν, ἢ Κάλαϊς.

CCIII ΣΤΡΑΤΩΝΟΣ

Οὐκ ἐθέλοντα φιλεῖς με, φιλῶ δ᾽ ἐγὼ οὐκ ἐθέλοντα
εὔκολος ἢν φεύγω, δύσκολος ἢν ἐπάγω.

CXCIX   STRATO

I've had enough to drink; my heart and soul
As well as tongue are losing self-control.
The lamp flame bifurcates; I multiply
The dinner guests by two each time I try.
Not only shaken up by the wine-waiter,
I ogle too the boy who pours the water.

CC   STRATO

I loathe a boy who won't be hugged and kissed,
Raises his voice and hits me with his fist,
Nor do I wish the wanton willingness
Of one who in my arms at once says, Yes.
I like one in between who seems to know
The secret of saying at once Yes and No.

CCI   STRATO

If pretty soon the rogue does not appear,
        I swear Cleonicus may stay away.
Why swear? He had a dream, but he'll be here
        Tomorrow. We'll survive another day.

CCII   STRATO

As soon as I saw your letter, Damis, saying
        That you were coming, Love blew me so fast
From Smyrna to Sardis, that the winds, relaying
        Each other, surely would have come in last.

CCIII   STRATO

You kiss me against my will, as I do you,
Pleasant when spurned, unpleasant when I woo.

CCIV ΣΤΡΑΤΩΝΟΣ

"Χρύσεα χαλκείων" νῦν εἴπατε· "δὸς λάβε" παίζει
Σωσιάδας ὁ καλός, καὶ Διοκλῆς ὁ δασύς.
τίς κάλυκας συνέκρινε βάτῳ, τίς σῦκα μύκησιν;
ἄρνα γαλακτοπαγῆ τίς συνέκρινε βοΐ;
οἷα δίδως, ἀλόγιστε, καὶ ἔμπαλιν οἷα κομίζῃ·
οὕτω Τυδείδης Γλαῦκον ἐδωροδόκει.

CCV ΣΤΡΑΤΩΝΟΣ

Παῖς τις ὅλως ἁπαλὸς τοῦ γείτονος οὐκ ὀλίγως με
κνίζει· πρὸς τὸ θέλειν δ᾽ οὐκ ἀμύητα γελᾷ·
οὐ πλεῦν δ᾽ ἐστὶν ἐτῶν δύο καὶ δέκα. νῦν ἀφύλακτοι
ὄμφακες· ἢν δ᾽ ἀκμάσῃ, φρούρια καὶ σκόλοπες.

CCVI ΣΤΡΑΤΩΝΟΣ

α. Ἦν τούτῳ †φωνῆς, τὸ μέσον λάβε, καὶ κατακλίνας!
ζεύγνυε, καὶ πρωσας πρόσπεσε, καὶ κάτεχε.
β. Οὐ φρονέεις, Διόφαντε· μόλις δύναμαι γὰρ ἔγωγε
ταῦτα ποιεῖν· παίδων δ᾽ ἡ πάλη ἔσθ᾽ ἑτέρα.
μοχλοῦ καὶ μένε, Κῦρι, καὶ ἐμβάλλοντος ἀνάσχου·
πρῶτον συμμελετᾶν ἢ μελετᾶν μαθέτω.

CCVII ΣΤΡΑΤΩΝΟΣ

Ἐχθὲς λουόμενος Διοκλῆς ἀνενήνοχε σαύραν
ἐκ τῆς ἐμβάσεως τὴν Ἀναδυομένην.
ταύτην εἴ τις ἔδειξεν Ἀλεξάνδρῳ τοτ᾽ ἐν Ἴδῃ,
τὰς τρεῖς ἂν ταύτης προκατέκρινε θεάς.

CCVIII ΣΤΡΑΤΩΝΟΣ

Εὐτυχές, οὐ φθονέω, βιβλίδιον· ἦ ῥά σ᾽ ἀναγνοὺς
παῖς τις ἀναθλίψει, πρὸς τὰ γένεια τιθείς·

97

CCIV STRATO

Were downy Diocles to trade his ass
For Sosiades', he'd get gold for brass,
Roses for brambles, figs for toadstools, or
A lamb for an ox. And what did you get for
Your favours, foolish boy? The pleasures had
By hairy heroes in the *Iliad*!

CCV STRATO

The kid next door exites me, with his bold,
    Enticing glances and precocious snigger—
Although he is no more than twelve years old!
    Green fruit grows free. He'll be locked up when bigger!

CCVI STRATO

A. To start with, grapple your opponent round
The waist, bestride and pin him to the ground.
B. You're mad! For that I'm hardly competent,
Wrestling with boys is something different.
Withstand my onslaught, Cyris, hold your own!
Let's practice together what you do alone.

CCVII STRATO

Yesterday in the bath Diocles' penis
Rose from the water like *The Birth of Venus*.
On Ida, if he'd sprung this same surprise,
Paris would have given it the prize.

CCVIII STRATO

I do not, little book, begrudge your luck,
Should any adolescent reader tuck

ἢ τρυφεροῖς σφίγξει περὶ χείλεσιν, ἢ κατὰ μηρῶν
εἰλήσει δροσερῶν, ὦ μακαριστότατον·
πολλάκι φοιτήσεις ὑποκόλπιον, ἢ παρὰ δίφρους
βληθὲν τολμήσεις κεῖνα θιγεῖν ἀφόβως.
πολλὰ δ᾿ ἐν ἠρεμίῃ προλαλήσεις· ἀλλ᾿ ὑπὲρ ἡμῶν,
χαρτάριον, δέομαι, πυκνότερόν τι λάλει.

CCIX   ΣΤΡΑΤΩΝΟΣ

Μήτε λίην στυγνὸς παρακέκλισο, μήτε κατηφής,
Δίφιλε, μηδ᾿ εἴης παιδίον ἐξ ἀγέλης.
ἔστω που προύνικα φιλήματα, καὶ τὰ πρὸ ἔργων
παίγνια, πληκτισμοί, κνίσμα, φίλημα, λόγος.

CCX   ΣΤΡΑΤΩΝΟΣ

Τρεῖς ἀρίθμει τοὺς πάντας ὑπὲρ λέχος, ὧν δύο δρῶσιν,
καὶ δύο πάσχουσιν. θαῦμα δοκῶ τι λέγειν.
καὶ μὴν οὐ ψεῦδος· δυσὶν εἰς μέσσος γὰρ ὑπουργεῖ
τέρτων ἐξόπιθεν, πρόσθε δὲ τερπόμενος.

CCXI   ΣΤΡΑΤΩΝΟΣ

Εἰ μὲν ἔφυς ἀμύητος ἀκμὴν ὑπὲρ οὗ σ᾿ ἔτι πείθω,
ὀρθῶς ἂν δείσαις, δεινὸν ἴσως δοκέων.
εἰ δέ σε δεσποτικὴ κοίτη πεποίηκε τεχνίτην,
τί φθονέεις δοῦναι, ταὐτὸ λαβών, ἑτέρῳ;
ὃς μὲν γὰρ καλέσας ἐπὶ τὸ χρέος, εἶτ᾿ ἀπολύσας,
εὕδει κύριος ὤν, μηδὲ λόγου μεταδούς·
ἄλλη δ᾿ ἔνθα τρυφή· παίξεις ἴσα, κοινὰ λαλήσεις,
τἄλλα δ᾿ ἐρωτηθεὶς κοὐκ ἐπιτασσόμενος.

CCXII   ΣΤΡΑΤΩΝΟΣ

Αἰαῖ μοι· τι πάλιν δεδακρυμενον, ἢ τι κατηφές,
παιδίον; εἶπον ἁπλῶς· μηδ᾿ ὀδύνα· τί θέλεις;

You under his chin, or nibble you, or press
You with his hairless thighs—what happiness!
How often you would sidle next his heart,
Or, dropped on a seat, dare touch a certain part!
You speak to him in private frequently,
Slim volume; now and then please speak of me.

CCIX   STRATO

Don't lie there at my side inert and glum,
        Diphilus, like a kid who's gone astray.
What about some kisses, cuddles, some
        Pillow talk and amorous foreplay?

CCX   STRATO

Three in one bed: while two are being done
        Two are doing them. Resolve this riddle.
        Strange but true: the fellow in the middle
In front and in behind is having fun.

CCXI   STRATO

Were you a novice I'd tried to persuade
To vice, you might be right to be afraid;
But since your master's bed taught you a lot,
Why not treat someone else to what you've got?
Called to your post, your duty done, without
A word, your sleepy master throws you out.
But here are other pleasures, free speech and
Fun by solicitation not command.

CCXII   STRATO

What now, my pet, depressed, in tears again?
What do you want? Don't torture me! Speak plain.

τὴν χέρα μοι κοίλην προσενήνοχας· ὡς ἀπόλωλα·
μισθὸν ἴσως αἰτεῖς· τοῦτ' ἔμαθες δὲ πόθεν;
οὐκέτι σοι κοπτῆς φίλιαι πλάκες οὐδὲ μελιχρὰ
σήσαμα, καὶ καρύων παίγνιος εὐστοχίη·
ἀλλ' ἤδη πρὸς κέρδος ἔχεις φρένας. ὡς ὁ διδάξας
τεθνάτω· οἶν μου παιδίον ἠφάνικεν.

CCXIII   ΣΤΡΑΤΩΝΟΣ

Τῷ τοίχῳ κέκλικας τὴν ὀσφύα τὴν περίβλεπτον,
Κῦρι· τί πειράζεις τὸν λίθον; οὐ δύναται.

CCXIV   ΣΤΡΑΤΩΝΟΣ

Δός μοι, καὶ λάβε χαλκόν. ἐρεῖς ὅτι "Πλούσιός εἰμι·"
δώρησαι τοίνυν τὴν χάριν, ὡς βασιλεύς.

CCXV   ΣΤΡΑΤΩΝΟΣ

Νῦν ἔαρ εἶ, μετέπειτα θέρος· κἄπειτα τί μέλλεις
Κῦρις; βούλευσαι, καὶ καλάμη γὰρ ἔσῃ.

CCXVI   ΣΤΡΑΤΩΝΟΣ

Νῦν ὀρθή, κατάρατε, καὶ εὔτονος, ἡνίκα μηδέν·
ἡνίκα δ' ἦν ἐχθές, οὐδὲν ὅλως ἀνέπνεις.

CCXVII   ΣΤΡΑΤΩΝΟΣ

Ἤδη ἐπὶ στρατιῆς ὁρμᾷς, ἔτι παῖς ἀδαὴς ὢν
καὶ τρυφερός. τί ποιεῖς, οὗτος, ὅρα· μετάθου.
οἴμοι· τίς σ' ἀνέπεισε λαβεῖν δόρυ· τίς χερὶ πέλτην;
τίς κρύψαι ταύτην τὴν κεφαλὴν κόρυθι;
ὦ μακαριστὸς ἐκεῖνος, ὅτις ποτέ, καινὸς Ἀχιλλεὺς
τοίῳ ἐνὶ κλισίῃ τερπόμενος Πατρόκλῳ.

You hold your palm out! I'm disgusted at
Your asking payment. Where did you learn that?
Seed cakes and conkers will not make you merry
Now, that your mind has grown so mercenary.
I curse the customer with his perverse
Lessons who made my little rascal worse!

CCXIII   STRATO

Against a wall you lean your fundament,
Cyris. Why tempt the stone? It's impotent.

CCXIV   STRATO

You'd say, "I'm rich!", if you sold me the thing
I crave. Now grant it freely, like a king.

CCXV   STRATO

Now Spring, you will be Summer soon. Recall,
Cyris, how you'll be stubble in the Fall.

CCXVI   STRATO

In solitude, you prick, you lift your head,
Who yesterday in company played dead.

CCXVII   STRATO

You're off to join the army? Such a nice
Mama's boy should think about it twice.
Who prompted you to wear a helmet, wield
A spear and hide your head behind a shield?
Lucky that new Achilles who will spend
Time in his tent with such a bossom friend!

CCXVIII   ΣΤΡΑΤΩΝΟΣ

Μέχρι τίνος σε γελῶντα μόνον, μηδὲν δὲ λαλοῦντα
οἴσομεν; εἶπον ἁπλῶς ταῦτα σύ, Πασίφιλε.
αἰτῶ, καὶ σὺ γελᾷς· πάλιν αἰτῶ, κοὺκ ἀποκρίνῃ·
δακρύω, σὺ γελᾷς. βάρβαρε, τοῦτο γέλως;

CCXIX   ΣΤΡΑΤΩΝΟΣ

Καὶ μισθοὺς αἰτεῖτε, διδάσκαλοι; ὡς ἀχάριστοι
ἐστέ· τί γάρ; τὸ βλέπειν παιδία μικρὸν ἴσως;
καὶ τούτοισι λαλεῖν, ἀσπαζομένους τε φιλῆσαι;
τοῦτο μόνον χρυσῶν ἄξιον οὐχ ἑκατόν;
πεμπέτω, εἴ τις ἔχει καλὰ παιδία· κἀμὲ φιλείτω,
μισθὸν καὶ παρ᾽ ἐμοῦ λαμβανέτω τί θέλει.

CCXX   ΣΤΡΑΤΩΝΟΣ

Οὐχὶ τὸ πῦρ κλέψας δέδεσαι, κακόβουλε Προμηθεῦ,
ἀλλ᾽ ὅτι τὸν πηλὸν τοῦ Διὸς ἠφάνισας.
πλάττων ἀνθρώπους, ἔβαλες τρίχας· ἔνθεν ὁ δεινὸς
πώγων, καὶ κνήμη παισὶ δασυνομένη.
εἶτά σε δαρδάπτει Διὸς αἰετός, ὃς Γανυμήδην
ἥρπασ᾽· ὁ γὰρ πώγων καὶ Διός ἐστ᾽ ὀδύνη.

CCXXI   ΣΤΡΑΤΩΝΟΣ

Στεῖχε πρὸς αἰθέρα δῖον, ἀπέρχεο παῖδα κομίζων,
αἰετέ, τὰς διφυεῖς ἐκπετάσας πτέρυγας,
στεῖχε τὸν ἁβρὸν ἔχων Γανυμήδεα, μηδὲ μεθείης
τὸν Διὸς ἡδίστων οἰνοχόον κυλίκων·
φείδεο δ᾽ αἱμάξαι κοῦρον γαμψώνυχι ταρσῷ,
μὴ Ζεὺς ἀλγήσῃ, τοῦτο βαρυνόμενος.

CCXVIII   STRATO

Tell me, Pasiphilus, how long must I
    Endure your laughter and your vapid chatter?
I ask, you laugh; again, and no reply.
    You laugh at my tears, which are no laughing matter.

CCXIX   STRATO

Ungrateful teachers, you want money, too?
Isn't the sight of boys enough for you?
Is chatting up and greeting your young scholars
With a kiss not worth a hundred dollars?
If you have winning kids, send them to me;
And if they'll kiss me they can name their fee.

CCXX   STRATO

Prometheus, for spiriting away
Fire are you bound, or marring mortal clay?
You gave boys body hairs, the horrid basis
Of fuzzy shanks and, what's worse, fuzzy faces.
Therefore you feed the eagle that once bore
Off Ganymede. Zeus too finds beards a bore.

CCXXI   STRATO

O eagle, flap your widespread wings and fly
Conveying Ganymede to Zeus's sky.
Grip tight the tender youth and don't let fall
The server of his sweetest drinks of all.
Be careful you don't scratch him with your claws,
Or Zeus will be annoyed, and with just cause.

CCXXII   ΣΤΡΑΤΩΝΟΣ

Εὐκαίρως ποτὲ παιδοτρίβης, λεῖον προδιδάσκων,
   εἰς τὸ γόνυ γνάμψας, μέσσον ἐπαιδοτρίβει,
τῇ χερὶ τοὺς κόκκους ἐπαφώμενος. ἀλλὰ τυχαίως
   τοῦ παιδὸς χρήζων, ἦλθεν ὁ δεσπόσυνος·
ὃς δὲ τάχος τοῖς ποσσὶν ὑποζώσας ἀνέκλινεν
   ὕπτιον, ἐμπλέξας τῇ χερὶ τὴν φάρυγα.
ἀλλ᾽ οὐκ ὢν ἀπάλαιστος ὁ δεσπόσυνος προσέειπεν·
   "Παῦσαι· πνιγίζεις," φησί, "τὸ παιδάριον."

CCXXIII   ΣΤΡΑΤΩΝΟΣ

Τερπνὸν ὅλως τὸ πρόσωπον ἐμοὶ προσιόντος ἀπαρκεῖ·
   οὐκέτι δ᾽ ἐξόπιθεν καὶ παριόντα βλέπω.
οὕτω γὰρ καὶ ἄγαλμα θεοῦ καὶ νηὸν ὁρῶμεν
   ἀντίον, οὐ πάντως καὶ τὸν ὀπισθόδομον.

CCXXIV   ΣΤΡΑΤΩΝΟΣ

Εἰς ἀγαθὴν συνέβημεν ἀταρπιτόν, ἣν ἀπὸ πρώτης
   φράζευ ὅπως ἔσται, Δίφιλε, καὶ μονίμη.
ἄμφω γὰρ πτηνόν τι λελόγχαμεν· ἔστι μὲν ἐν σοὶ
   κάλλος, ἔρως δ᾽ ἐν ἐμοί· καίρια δ᾽ ἀμφότερα.
ἄρτι μὲν ἁρμοσθέντα μένει χρόνον· εἰ δ᾽ ἀφύλακτα
   μίμνετον ἀλλήλων, ᾤχετ᾽ ἀποπτάμενα.

CCXXV   ΣΤΡΑΤΩΝΟΣ

Οὐδέποτ᾽ ἡελίου φάος ὄρθριον ἀντέλλοντος
   μίσγεσθαι ταύρῳ χρὴ φλογόεντα κύνα,
μή ποτε καρπολόχου Δήμητρος ὑγρανθείσης,
   βρέξῃς τὴν λασίην Ἡρακλέους ἄλοχον.

CCXXII   STRATO

A wrestling coach who'd bent a hairless lad
Over his knee, to stroke his midriff, had
Him by the nuts, when, seeking the little guy,
The head of the establishment chanced by.
The trainer flipped his pupil on his back,
Bestrode him, and put his hands around his neck,
Quickly. His boss, who knew a trick or two,
Said, "Squeezing the kid a little hard, aren't you?"

CCXXIII   STRATO

A boy looks so charming as he faces you,
      You don't gaze at his backside as you pass;
As in a temple when we face a statue
      We seldom bother to inspect its ass.

CCXXIV   STRATO

Together down the primrose path we go,
And, Diphilus, take care to keep it so.
We both boast high-flown qualities: you glory
In beauty, I in love—each transitory:
A little while in tandem lingering,
Once they forget each other they take wing.

CCXXV   STRATO

At cock crow there is never any need
      To do it doggy style or milk the bull,
Or to besprinkle with your liquid seed
      Your Ganymede's pubescent patch of wool.

106

CCXXVI   ΣΤΡΑΤΩΝΟΣ

Πάννυχα μυδαλόεντα πεφυρμένος ὄμματα κλαυθμῷ
ἄγρυπνον ἀμπαύω θυμὸν ἀδημονίῃ,
ἤ με κατ᾽ οὖν ἐδάμασσεν ἀποζευχθέντος ἑταίρου,
μοῦνον ἐπεί με λιπὼν εἰς ἰδίην Ἔφεσον
χθιζὸς ἔβη Θεόδωρος· ὃς εἰ πάλι μὴ ταχὺς ἔλθοι,
οὐκέτι μουνολεχεῖς κοίτας ἀνεξόμεθα.

CCXXVII   ΣΤΡΑΤΩΝΟΣ

Ἤν τινα καὶ παριδεῖν ἐθέλω καλὸν ἀντισυναντῶν,
βαιὸν ὅσον παραβὰς εὐθὺ μεταστρέφομαι.

CCXXVIII   ΣΤΡΑΤΩΝΟΣ

Παῖδα μὲν ἡλιτόμηνον ἐς ἄφρονα καιρὸν ἁμαρτεῖν,
τῷ πείθοντι φέρει πλεῖον ὕβρισμα φίλῳ.
ἤδη δ᾽ ἐν νεότητι παρήλικα παιδικὰ πάσχειν,
τῷ παρέχοντι πάλιν τοῦτο δὶς αἰσχρότερον.
ἔστι δ᾽ ὅτ᾽ ἀμφοτέροις τὸ μὲν οὐκέτι, Μοῖρι, τὸ δ᾽ οὔπω
ἀπρεπές, οἷον ἐγὼ καὶ σὺ τὸ νῦν ἔχομεν.

CCXXIX   ΣΤΡΑΤΩΝΟΣ

Ὡς ἀγαθὴ θεός ἐστι, δι᾽ ἥν ὑπὸ κόλπον, Ἄλεξι,
πτύομεν, ὑστερόπουν ἁζόμενοι Νέμεσιν.
ἣν σὺ μετερχομένην οὐκ ἔβλεπες, ἀλλ᾽ ἐνόμιζες
ἕξειν τὸ φθονερὸν κάλλος ἀειχρόνιον.
νῦν δὲ τὸ μὲν διόλωλεν· ἐλήλυθε δ᾽ ἡ τριχάλεπτος
δαίμων· χοὶ θέραπες νῦν σε παρερχόμεθα.

CCXXVI   STRATO

All night long I wipe my weeping eyes
And soothe my sleepless soul that wakes and cries
For Theodore, my friend who went away
And left me all alone here yesterday.
He swore he'd soon be back; if he is late,
I can not long continue celibate.

CCXXVII   STRATO

Although I will not meet a cute boy's eye,
I turn around as soon as I pass by.

CCXXVIII   STRATO

If any minor foolishly consents
We blame the corrupter of his innocence.
But once a youth has outgrown child's play, it
Is twice as shameful for him to submit.
But there's a time when it's not yet too late
Moeris, or too soon, to celebrate.

CCXXIX   STRATO

How good, Alexis, is that Nemesis,
To check whose dread advance we spit like this!
You did not see her coming, thinking your
Invidious beauty yours for evermore,
Since ruined by harsh hairs. And that is why
We, once your followers, now pass you by.

108

CCXXX ΚΑΛΛΙΜΑΧΟΥ

Τὸν τὸ καλὸν μελανεῦντα Θεόκριτον, εἰ μὲν ἔμ' ἔχθει,
τετράκι μισοίης· εἰ δὲ φιλεῖ, φιλέοις·
ναίχι πρὸς εὐχαίτεω Γανυμήδεος, οὐράνιε Ζεῦ,
καὶ σὺ ποτ' ἠράσθης. οὐκέτι μακρὰ λέγω.

CCXXXI ΣΤΡΑΤΩΝΟΣ

Εὐκλείδῃ φιλέοντι πατὴρ θάνεν· ἃ μάκαρ αἰει,
καὶ πρὶν ἐς ὅττι φέλοι χρηστὸν ἔχων πατέρα
καὶ νῦν εὔφρονα νεκρόν. ἐγὼ δ' ἔτι λάθρια παίζω·
φεῦ μοίρης τε κακῆς καὶ πατρὸς ἀθανάτου.

CCXXXII ΣΚΥΘΙΝΟΥ

Ὀρθὸν νῦν ἔστηκας ἀνώνυμον οὐδὲ μαραίνῃ,
ἐντέτασαι δ' ὡς ἂν μή ποτε παυσόμενον·
ἀλλ' ὅτε μοι Νεμεσηνὸς ὅλον παρέκλινεν ἑαυτόν,
πάντα διδοὺς ἃ θέλω, νεκρὸν ἀπεκρέμασο.
τείνεο, καὶ ῥήσσου, καὶ δάκρυε· πάντα ματαίως,
οὐχ ἕξεις ἔλεον χειρὸς ἀφ' ἡμετέρης.

CCXXXIII ΦΡΟΝΤΩΝΟΣ

Τὴν ἀκμὴν Θησαυρὸν ἔχειν, κωμῳδέ, νομίζεις,
οὐκ εἰδὼς αὐτὴν Φάσματος ὀξυτέρην.
ποιήσει σ' ὁ χρόνος Μισούμενον, εἶτα Γεωργόν,
καὶ τότε μαστεύσεις τὴν Περικειρομένην.

CCXXXIV ΣΤΡΑΤΩΝΟΣ

Εἰ κάλλει καυχᾷ, γίνωσχ' ὅτι καὶ ῥόδον ἀνθεῖ·
ἀλλὰ μαρανθὲν ἄφνω σὺν κοπρίοις ἐρίφη.
ἄνθος γὰρ καὶ κάλλος ἴσον χρόνον ἐστὶ λαχόντα·
ταῦτα δ' ὁμῇ φθονέων ἐξεμάρανε χρόνος.

CCXXX   CALLIMACHUS

If, Zeus in heaven! dark Theocritus
Dislikes me, judge him twice as odious.
But if he cares for me, befriend him. Need
I cite your love for fair-haired Ganymede?

CCXXXI   STRATO

Euclid in love is lucky. His dad died.
    In life this kindly corpse indulged whatever
His son desired. Still I am doomed to hide
    My pleasures—my old man will live forever.

CCXXXII   SCYTHINUS

Erect you stand now, thingamajig, as if
You'd never quit, so vigorous and stiff.
When Nemesenus snuggled up in bed,
Indulging my every whim, you hung your head.
Now swollen fit to burst you weep in vain:
My hand will not take mercy on your pain.

CCXXXIII   FRONTO

The role of your lifetime was *My Secret Garden,*
    You thought, but it is *Gone with the Wind* now, boy.
After *Stand by Me,* you'll play *Flesh Gordon,*
    And soon you'll be rehearsing *Midnight Cowboy.*

CCXXXIV   STRATO

You vaunt your beauty; you know roses flower,
    Wither, and are thrown out on the midden.
Beauty and bloom which share a given hour
    By grasping time are equally hag-ridden.

110

CCXXXV   ΣΤΡΑΤΩΝΟΣ

Εἰ μὲν γηράσκει τὸ καλόν, μετάδος, πρὶν ἀπέλθῃ·
εἰ δὲ μένει, τί φοβῇ τοῦθ' ὃ μενεῖ διδόναι;

CCXXXVI   ΣΤΡΑΤΩΝΟΣ

Εὐνοῦχός τις ἔχει καλὰ παιδία· πρὸς τίνα χρῆσιν;
καὶ τούτοισι βλάβην οὐχ ὁσίην παρέχει.
ὄντως ὡς ὁ κύων φάτνῃ ῥόδα, μωρὰ δ' ὑλακτῶν
οὔθ' αὑτῷ παρέχει τἀγαθόν, οὔθ' ἑτέρῳ.

CCXXXVII   ΣΤΡΑΤΩΝΟΣ

Χαῖρε σύ, μισοπόνηρε πεπλασμένε, χαῖρε, βάναυσε
ὁ πρῴην ὀμόσας μηκέτι μὴ διδόναι.
μηκέτι νῦν ὀμόσῃς. ἔγνωκα γάρ, οὐδέ με λήθεις·
οἶδα τὸ ποῦ, καὶ πῶς, καὶ τίνι, καὶ τὸ πόσου.

CCXXXVIII   ΣΤΡΑΤΩΝΟΣ

Ἀλλήλοις παρέχουσιν ἀμοιβαδίην ἀπόλαυσιν
οἱ κύνεοι πῶλοι μειρακιευόμενοι·
ἀμφαλλὰξ δὲ οἱ αὐτοὶ ἀπόστροφα νωτοβατοῦνται,
τὸ δρᾶν καὶ τὸ παθεῖν ἀντιπεραινόμενοι.
οὐ πλεονεκτεῖται δ' οὐδ' ἅτερος· ἄλλοτε μὲν γὰρ
ἵσταται ὁ προδιδοὺς ἄλλοτ' ὄπισθε πάλιν.
τοῦτ' ἐστὶν πάντως τὸ προοίμιον· εἰς γὰρ ἀμοιβήν,
ὡς λέγεται, κνήθειν οἶδεν ὄνος τὸν ὄνον.

CCXXXIX   ΣΤΡΑΤΩΝΟΣ

Πέντ' αἰτεῖς, δέκα δώσω· ἐείκοσι δ' †ἀντία ἕξεις.
ἀρκεῖ σοι χρυσοῦς; ἤρκεσε καὶ Δανάῃ.

CCXXXV   STRATO

If beauty spoils, share it before it's spent;
If not, why fear to give what's permanent?

CCXXXVI   STRATO

A eunuch has cute slaveboys. What's the use?
Can he subject them to profane abuse?
A dog in the manger, barking to annoy,
He spoils for others what he can't enjoy.

CCXXXVII   STRATO

Fuck off, you hypocrite, you little lout!
You swore that nevermore would you put out.
Don't swear again; I'm not deceived by you:
I know with whom, where, how—for how much, too.

CCXXXVIII   STRATO

In their erotic play with one another
    Puppies give and take a lot of pleasure:
Reciprocally mounted by each other,
    They screw as they are screwed, measure for measure.
The underdog—for no one is left out—
    Immediately to the rear will pass.
So in the proverb: turn and turn about,
    It's said, it takes an ass to scratch an ass.

CCXXXIX   STRATO

You ask for five, I'll give you ten, or twenty.
Is gold enough? For Danae it was plenty.

112

CCXL   ΣΤΡΑΤΩΝΟΣ

Ἤδη μοι πολιαὶ μὲν ἐπὶ κροτάφοισιν ἔθειραι,
    καὶ πέος ἐν μηροῖς ἀργὸν ἀποκρέμαται·
ὄρχεις δ' ἄπρηκτοι, χαλεπὸν δέ με γῆρας ἱκάνει.
    οἴμοι· πυγίζειν οἶδα, καὶ οὐ δύναμαι.

CCXLI   ΣΤΡΑΤΩΝΟΣ

Ἄγκιστρον πεπόηκας, ἔχεις ἰχθὺν ἐμέ, τέκνον·
    ἕλκε μ' ὅπου βούλει· μὴ τρέχε, μή σε φύγω.

CCXLII   ΣΤΡΑΤΩΝΟΣ

Πρώην τὴν σαύραν ῥοδοδάκτυλον, Ἄλκιμ', ἔδειξας·
    νῦν αὐτὴν ἤδη καὶ ῥοδόπηχυν ἔχεις.

CCXLIII   ΣΤΡΑΤΩΝΟΣ

Εἴ με τὸ πυγίζειν ἀπολώλεκε, καὶ διὰ τοῦτο
    †ἐκτρέφομαι ποδαγρῶν, Ζεῦ, κρεάγραν με πόει.

CCXLIV   ΣΤΡΑΤΩΝΟΣ

Ἢν ἐσίδω τινὰ λευκόν, ἀπόλλυμαι· ἢν δὲ μελίχρουν,
    καίομαι· ἢν ξανθὸν δ', εὐθὺς ὅλος λέλυμαι.

CCXLV   ΣΤΡΑΤΩΝΟΣ

Πᾶν ἄλογον ζῷον βινεῖ μόνον· οἱ λογικοὶ δὲ
    τῶν ἄλλων ζῴων τοῦτ' ἔχομεν τὸ πλέον,
πυγίζειν εὑρόντες. ὅσοι δὲ γυναιξὶ κρατοῦνται,
    τῶν ἀλόγων ζῴων οὐδὲν ἔχουσι πλέον.

CCXL   STRATO

Already on my head the hairs grow white,
    Between my thighs my doodle dangles too;
My balls are useless. Old age looms in sight.
    Though I know how, I can no longer screw.

CCXLI   STRATO

You've baited your hook and caught me, child. You may
Tug as you like, but don't run, or I'll get away.

CCXLII   STRATO

Your rosy fingered prick that used to charm
Us, Alcimus, is now a rosy arm.

CCXLIII   STRATO

Ass-fucking ruined me and made me limp:
Though gouty, good God forbid I should go limp!

CCXLIV   STRATO

A milk-white boy undoes me at first sight;
A honey-coloured lad sets me alight;
A golden boy, however, melts me quite.

CCXLV   STRATO

Dumb brutes only fuck; we clever human
    Beings, in this superior at least,
Invented buggery. The slaves of women
    Have no more sophistication than a beast.

114

CCXLVI   ΣΤΡΑΤΩΝΟΣ

Ζεῦγος ἀδελφειῶν με φιλεῖ. οὐκ οἶδα τίν᾽ αὐτῶν
δεσπόσυνον κρίνω· τοὺς δύο γὰρ φιλέω.
χὠ μὲν ἀποστείχει, ὁ δ᾽ ἐπέρχεται· ἔστι δὲ τοῦ μὲν
κάλλιστον τὸ παρόν, τοῦ δὲ τὸ λειπόμενον.

CCXLVII   ΣΤΡΑΤΩΝΟΣ

Οἷον ἐπὶ Τροίῃ ποτ᾽ ἀπὸ Κρήτης, Θεόδωρε,
Ἰδομενεὺς θεράποντ᾽ ἤγαγε Μηριόνην,
τοῖον ἔχω σε φίλον περιδέξιον. ἦ γὰρ ἐκεῖνος
ἄλλα μὲν ἦν θεράπων, ἄλλα δ᾽ ἑταιρόσυνος·
καὶ σὺ τὰ μὲν βιότοιο πανήμερος ἔργα τέλει μοι·
νῦν δέ γε πειρῶμεν, ναὶ Δία, Μηριόνην.

CCXLVIII   ΣΤΡΑΤΩΝΟΣ

Τίς δύναται γνῶναι τὸν ἐρώμενον εἰ παρακμάζει,
πάντα συνὼν αὐτῷ μηδ᾽ ἀπολειπόμενος;
τίς δύνατ᾽ οὐκ ἀρέσαι τὴν σήμερον, ἐχθὲς ἀρέσκων;
εἰ δ᾽ ἀρέσει, τί παθὼν αὔριον οὐκ ἀρέσει;

CCXLIX   ΣΤΡΑΤΩΝΟΣ

Βουποίητε μέλισσα, πέθεν μέλι τοὐμὸν ἰδοῦσα
παιδὸς ἐφ᾽ ὑαλέην ὄψιν ὑπερπέτασαι;
οὐ παύσῃ βομβεῦσα, καὶ ἀνθολόγοισι θέλουσα
ποσσὶν ἐφάψασθαι χρωτὸς ἀκηροτάτου;
ἔρρ᾽ ἐπὶ σοὺς μελίπαιδας ὅποι ποτέ, δραπέτι, σίμ-βλους,
μή σε δάκω· κἠγὼ κέντρον ἔρωτος ἔχω.

CCL   ΣΤΡΑΤΩΝΟΣ

Νυκτερινὴν ἐπίκωμος ἰὼν μεταδόρπιον ὥρην
ἄρνα λύκος θυρέτροις εὗρον ἐφεσταότα,

CCXLVI   STRATO

Twins love me, and I do not know which brother
    To choose as overlord, for both I love.
    They come and go. I judge the absence of
One equal to the presence of the other.

CCXLVII   STRATO

As Idomeneus brought from Crete to Troy
Meriones to be his serving-boy,
I have a helpmeet, Theodore, in you,
Like him a servant and a playmate too.
Perform your household duties every day;
At night at squire and master let us play.

CCXLVIII   STRATO

Having your boy beside you all the time
How can you tell if he is past his prime?
Who, pleasing yesterday, will not today?
And if today, why not the following day?

CCXLIX   STRATO

Spying my honey, bully boy bee, why
Straight to his slick face in a bee line fly?
Buzz off! Stop trying to massage his sweet,
Unblemished skin with sticky little feet.
Go home to your honeyed boy-hive, flighty thing,
Or *I'll* sting *you*, with my erotic sting.

CCL   STRATO

As I set out carousing one night late,
A lucky wolf, I found a lambkin at my gate,

υἱὸν Ἀριστοδίκου τοῦ γείτονος· ὃν περιπλεχθεὶς
ἐξεφίλουν ὅρκοις πολλὰ χαριζόμενος.
νῦν δ' αὐτῷ τί φέρων δωρήσομαι; οὔτ' ἀπάτης γὰρ
ἄξιος, Ἑσπερίης οὔτ' ἐπιορκοσύνης.

CCLI   ΣΤΡΑΤΩΝΟΣ

Πρόσθε μὲν ἀντιπρόσωπα φιλήματα καὶ τὰ πρὸ πείρας
εἴχομεν· ἧς γὰρ ἀκμήν, Δίφιλε, παιδάριον.
νῦν δέ σε τῶν ὄπιφεν γουνάζομαι, οὐ παρεόντων
ὕστερον· ἔστω γὰρ πάντα καθ' ἡλικίην.

CCLII   ΣΤΡΑΤΩΝΟΣ

Ἐμπρήσω σε, θύρη, τῇ λαμπάδι, καὶ τὸν ἔνοικον
συμφλέξας μεθύων, εὐθὺς ἄπειμι φυγάς,
καὶ πλώσας Ἀδριανὸν ἐπ' οἴνοπα πόντον, ἀλήτης
φωλήσω γε θύραις νυκτὸς ἀνοιγομέναις.

CCLIII   ΣΤΡΑΤΩΝΟΣ

Δεξιτερὴν ὀλίγον δὸς ἐπὶ χρόνον, οὐχ ἵνα παύσῃς
(κεῖ μ' ὁ καλὸς χλεύην ἔσχε) χοροιτυπίης.
ἀλλ', εἰ μὴ πλευρῇ παρεκέκλιτο πατρὸς ἀκαίρως,
οὐκ ἂν δή με μάτην εἶδε μεθυσκόμενον.

CCLIV   ΣΤΡΑΤΩΝΟΣ

Ἐκ ποίου ναοῦ, πόθεν ὁ στόλος οὗτος Ἐρώτων,
πάντα καταστίλβων; ἄνδρες, ἀμαυρὰ βλέπω.
τίς τούτων δοῦλος, τίς ἐλεύθερος; οὐ δύναμ' εἰπεῖν.
ἄνθρωπος τούτων κύριος; οὐ δύναται.
εἰ δ' ἐστίν, μείζων πολλῷ Διός, ὃς Γανυμήδην
ἔσχε μόνως, θεὸς ὢν πηλίκος· ὃς πόσους;

My neighbour's son. I kissed and hugged him tight,
And promised him plenty in my heart's delight.
What shall I give him? He's too sweet to cheat,
Or hoodwink with slick, Italianate deceit.

CCLI   STRATO

Foreplay and kisses face to face we had
When, Diphilus, you were a little lad;
'Behind and out of mind', I now assuage,
Kneeling, my passing passion. Act your age.

CCLII   STRATO

I'll burn the door down with a fiery brand
      And roast the boy inside. Then I'll take flight
Over the wine-dark Adriatic and
      Watch at some door that opens up at night.

CCLIII   STRATO

Give me a hand, but not to stop me, friend,
      Cavorting. Were that cheeky boy not tied
      Unfortunately to his father's side,
He wouldn't find me tipsy to no end.

CCLIV   STRATO

Out of what shrine, bedazzling my sight,
Issues this band of Loves diffusing light?
Which is a slave and which a gentleman?
Their lord can hardly be a mortal man,
Greater than Zeus, for while Zeus hasn't any
Catamite but Ganymede, he has so many!

118

CCLV ΣΤΡΑΤΩΝΟΣ

Οὐδ᾿ αὕτη σ᾿ ἡ λέξις, ἀκοινώνητε, διδάσκει,
ἐξ ἐτύμου φωνῆς ῥήμασιν ἑλκομένη;
πᾶς φιλόπαις λέγεται, Διονύσιε, κοὐ φιλοβούπαις.
πρὸς τοῦτ᾿ ἀντειπεῖν μή τι πάλιν δύνασαι;
Πύθι᾿ ἀγωνοθετῶ, σὺ δ᾿ Ὀλύμπια· χοῦς ἀποβάλλων
ἐκκρίνω, τούτους εἰς τὸν ἀγῶνα δέχῃ.

CCLVI ΜΕΛΕΑΓΡΟΥ

Παγκαρπόν σοι, Κύπρι, καθήρμοσε, χειρὶ τρυγήσας
παίδων ἄνθος, Ἔρως ψυχαπάτην στέφανον.
ἐν μὲν γὰρ κρίνον ἡδὺ κατέπλεξεν Διόδωρον,
ἐν δ᾿ Ἀσκληπιάδην, τὸ γλυκὺ λευκόϊον.
ναὶ μὴν Ἡράκλειτον ἐπέπλεκεν, ὡς ἀπ᾿ ἀκάνθης
†εἰς ῥόδον,¹ οἰνάνθη δ᾿ ὥς τις ἔθαλλε Δίων·
χρυσάνθη δὲ κόμαισι κρόκον Θήρωνα συνῆψεν·
ἐν δ᾿ ἔβαλ᾿ ἑρπύλλου κλωνίον Οὐλιάδην,
ἁβροκόμην δὲ Μυΐσκον, ἀειθαλὲς ἔρνος ἐλαίης·
ἱμερτοὺς δ᾿ Ἀρέτου κλῶνας ἀπεδρέπετο.
ὀλβίστη νήσων ἱερὰ Τύρος, ἣ τὸ μυρόπνουν
ἄλσος ἔχει παίδων Κύπριδος ἀνθοφόρον.

CCLVIII ΣΤΡΑΤΩΝΟΣ

Ἦ τάχα τις μετόπισθε κλύων ἐμὰ παίγνια ταῦτα,
πάντας ἐμοὺς δόξει τοὺς ἐν ἔρωτι πόνους·
ἄλλα δ᾿ ἐγὼν ἄλλοισιν ἀεὶ φιλόπαισι χαράσσω
γράμματ᾿, ἐπεί τις ἐμοὶ τοῦτ᾿ ἐνέδωκε θεός.

CCLV   STRATO

You maverick, what language should explain
The derivation of the word makes plain:
Boy-lovers, Dionysius, love boys—
You can't deny it—not great hobblehoys.
After I referee the Pythian
Games, you umpire the Olympian:
The failed contestants I once sent away
You welcome as competitors today.

CCLVI   MELEAGER

For Venus Love arranged a rich bouquet,
Of boys, hand-picked to steal the heart away,
And next to Diodorus' lily set
Asclepiades' sweet, white violet,
Let Heraclitus' thorny rose entwine
Dion like a blossom on the vine,
Shy Uliades' sprig of thyme beside
Resplendent Theron's saffron crocus hide;
And evergreen Myiscus' olive sprout
Aretus' lovely greenery tricks out.
O blessèd Tyre that boasts the perfumed grove
Of Venus where the cult of boy-love throve!

CCLVIII   STRATO

Some reader of this child's play in another
      Age may think these heart-throbs all were mine.
For writing different epigrams for other
      Lovers of boys my talent was divine.

CCLVII   ΜΕΛΕΑΓΡΟΥ

Ἁ πύματον καμπτῆρα καταγγέλλουσα κορωνίς,
ἑρκοῦρος γραπταῖς πιστοτάτα σελίσιν,
φαμὶ τὸν ἐκ πάντων ἠθροισμένον εἰς ἕνα μόχθον
ὑμνοθετᾶν βύβλῳ τᾷδ᾽ ἐνελιξάμενον
ἐκτελέσαι Μελέαγρον, ἀείμνηστον δὲ Διοκλεῖ
ἄνθεσι συμπλέξαι μουσοπόλον στέφανον.
                               οὖλα
εὐμαθίας.   δ᾽ ἐγὼ
τέρμασιν   καμφθεῖσα
    ἵδρυμαι   δρακοντείοις
    σύνθρονος   ἴσα
            νώτοις,

ANTHOLOGIA PALATINA, BOOK XI,

XLVIII   ΑΝΑΚΡΕΟΝΤΟΣ

Τὸν ἄργυρον τορεύσας
Ἥφαιστέ μοι ποίησον
πανοπλίαν μὲν οὐχί,
ποτήριον δὲ κοῖλον
ὅσον δύνῃ βάθυνον.
ποίει δέ μοι κατ᾽ αὐτοῦ
μηδ᾽ ἄστρα, μηδ᾽ ἁμάξας,
μὴ στυγνὸν Ὠρίωνα,
ἀλλ᾽ ἀμπέλους χλοώσας,
καὶ βότρυας γελῶντας,
σὺν τῷ καλῷ Λυαίῳ.

CCLVII   MELEAGER

As colophon that underlines The End,
Designed these written columns to defend,
I say first Meleager undertook
To gather many poets in one book,
Completing a verse garland twined from these
Memorable flowers for Diocles.

                              Coiled
        wit.   like
      of   a
    terminus   serpent
      the   on
        state,   myself
                  in here I sit

ANTHOLOGIA PALATINA, BOOK XI,

XLVIII   ANACREON

Hephaestus, silversmith,
Do not fashion me
Some warlike panoply,
But a hollow cup
Deep as it can be.
And decorate it with
No constellated stars
Or hateful armoured cars,
But a blooming vine
With bunches beaming up
At the bonny god of wine.

INDEX OF AUTHORS

(References are to the number of each poem.)

Statyllius Flaccus: XII, XXV, XXVI,
XXVII
Strato: I, II, III, IV, V, VI, VII, VIII, IX,
X, XI, XIII, XV, XXI, CLXXV,
CLXXVI, CLXXVII, CLXXVIII,
CLXXIX, CLXXX, CLXXXI,
CLXXXII, CLXXXIII, CLXXXIV,
CLXXXV, CLXXXVI, CLXXXVII,
CLXXXVIII, CLXXXIX, CXC,
CXCI, CXCII, CXCIII, CXCIV
CXCV, CXCVI, CXCVII, CXCVIII,
CXCIX, CC, CCI, CCII, CCIII,
CCIV, CCV, CCVI, CCVII,
CCVIII, CCIX CCX, CCXI,

CCXII, CCXIII, CCXIV, CCXV,
CCXVI, CCXVII, CCXVIII,
CCXIX, CCXXXI, CCXXXIV,
CCXXXV, CCXXXVI, CCXXXVII,
CCXXXVIII, CCXXXIX, CCXL,
CCXLI, CCXLII, CCXLIII,
CCXLIV, CCXLV, CCXLVI,
CCXLVII, CCXLVIII, CCXLIX,
CCL, CCLI, CCLII, CCLIII,
CCLIV, CCLV, CCLVIII

Thymocles: XXXII
Tullius Laureas: XXIV

THE LOCKERT LIBRARY OF POETRY IN TRANSLATION

George Seferis: Collected Poems (1924–1995), translated, edited, and introduced by Edmund Keeley and Philip Sherrard

Collected Poems of Lucio Piccolo, translated and edited by Brian Swann and Ruth Feldman

C. P. Cavafy: Selected Poems, translated by Edmund Keeley and Philip Sherrard and edited by George Savidis

Benny Andersen: Collected Poems, translated by Alexander Taylor

Selected Poetry of Andrea Zanzotto, edited and translated by Ruth Feldman and Brian Swann

Poems of René Char, translated and annotated by Mary Ann Caws and Jonathan Griffin

Selected Poems of Tudor Arghezi, translated by Michael Impey and Brian Swann

"The Survivor" and Other Poems by Tadeusz Różewicz, translated and introduced by Magnus J. Krynski and Robert A. Maguire

"Harsh World" and Other Poems by Angel González, translated by Donald D. Walsh

Ritsos in Parentheses, translations and introduction by Edmund Keeley

Salamander: Selected Poems by Robert Marteau, translated by Anne Winters

Angelos Sikelianos: Selected Poems, translated and introduced by Edmund Keeley and Philip Sherrard

Dante's "Rime," translated by Patrick S. Diehl

Selected Later Poems of Marie Luise Kaschnitz, translated by Lisel Mueller

Osip Mandelstam's "Stone," translated and introduced by Robert Tracy

The Dawn Is Always New: Selected Poetry of Rocco Scotellaro, translated by Ruth Feldman and Brian Swann

Sounds, Feelings, Thoughts: Seventy Poems by Widlawa Szymborska, translated and introduced by Magnus J. Krynski and Robert A. Maguire

The Man I Pretend to Be: "The Colloquies" and Selected Poems of Guido Gozzano, translated and edited by Michael Palma, with an introductory essay by Eugenio Montale

D'Après Tout: Poems by Jean Follain, translated by Heather McHugh

Songs of Something Else: Selected Poems of Gunnar Ekelöf, translated by Leonard Nathan and James Larson

The Little Treasury of One Hundred People, One Poem Each, compiled by Fujiwara No Sadaie and translated by Tom Galt

The Ellipse: Selected Poems of Leonardo Sinisgalli, translated by W. S. Di Piero

The Difficult Days by Roberto Sosa, translated by Jim Lindsey

Hymns and Fragments by Friedrich Hölderlin, translated and introduced by Richard Sieburth

The Silence Afterwards: Selected Poems of Rolf Jacobsen, translated and edited by Roger Greenwald

Rilke: Between Roots, selected poems rendered from the German by Rika Lesser

In the Storm of Roses: Selected Poems by Ingeborg Bachmann, translated, edited, and introduced by Mark Anderson

Birds and Other Relations: Selected Poetry of Dezső Tandori, translated by Bruce Berlind

Brocade River Poems: Selected Works of the Tang Dynasty Courtesan Xue Tao, translated and introduced by Jeanne Larsen

The True Subject: Selected Poems of Faiz Ahmed Faiz, translated by Naomi Lazard

My Name on the Wind: Selected Poems of Diego Valeri, translated by Michael Palma

Aeschylus: The Suppliants, translated by Peter Burian

Foamy Sky: The Major Poems of Miklós Radnóti, selected and translated by Zsuzsanna Ozváth and Frederick Turner

La Fontaine's Bawdy: Of Libertines, Louts, and Lechers, translated by Norman R. Shapiro

A Child Is Not a Knife: Selected Poems of Göran Sonnevi, translated and edited by Rika Lesser

George Seferis: Collected Poems, Revised Edition, translated, edited, and introduced by Edmund Keeley and Philip Sherrard

C. P. Cavafy: Collected Poems, Revised Edition, translated and introduced by Edmund Keeley and Philip Sherrard

Selected Poems of Shmuel HaNagid, translated from the Hebrew by Peter Cole

The Late Poems of Meng Chiao, translated by David Hinton

Leopardi: Selected Poems, translated by Eamon Gennan

Through Naked Branches: Selected Poems of Tarjei Vesaas, translated and edited by Roger Greenwald

The Complete Odes and Satires of Horace, translated with introduction and notes by Sidney Alexander

Selected Poems of Solomon Ibn Gabirol, translated by Peter Cole

Puerilities: Erotic Epigrams of The Greek Anthology, translated by Daryl Hine